Erweiterte Ausgabe D3

English G 21

Klassenarbeitstrainer

für Schülerinnen und Schüler

mit Lösungen und Lerntipps

Cornelsen

English G 21 • Band D 3 Erweiterte Ausgabe

Klassenarbeitstrainer mit Lösungen und Lerntipps

Konzeption
Dr. Ursula Mulla und Nogi Mulla, Germering

Erarbeitet von
Bärbel Schweitzer M.A., Staufen

In Zusammenarbeit mit der Englischredaktion
Dr. Christiane Kallenbach (Projektleitung)
Stefanie Bayer (verantwortliche Redakteurin)
Susanne Bennetreu, Ulrike Berendt (Bildredaktion)

Beratende Mitwirkung
Angela Ringel-Eichinger, Bietigheim-Bissingen
Martina Schroeder, Stedtlingen
Bernd Sold, Bobenheim-Roxheim

Illustrationen
Constanze Schargan, Berlin
Roland Beier, Berlin (S. 6, S. 26, S. 41/3)

Bildquellen
Corbis, Düsseldorf (S. 12 Bild 3: Norbert Schaefer; S. 17: Pixland; S. 47 unten li.: Envision; S. 58: Tom Steward; S. 59 li.: Stefanie Grewel/zefa/Corbis); blickwinkel, Witten (S. 14 Bild 4: F. Hecker); furryface (S. 10 unten); Getty, München (S. 30 oben re.: Rana Faure, S. 47 oben Mitte: Russell Kaye / Sandra-Lee Phipps); istockphoto, Calgary (S. 10 oben: Renars Jurkovskis; S. 15 Tower Bridge: Junghee Choi; S. 18 unten re.: Jane Norton; S. 26: Monique Rodriguez; S. 59 oben re.: Aleksej Vasic; unten re.: Tony Tremblay; S. 62 Lisa: Anastasia Bobrova; S. 64: Jasmin Awad); The Lowry, Salford Quays (S. 38 li.); The LS Lowry Collection, Salford (S. 38 re.); Nic McPhee, Minnesota (S. 47 unten re.); Picture Alliance, Frankfurt / Main (S. 12 Bild 5: Jens Wolf); www.pitlochry.org.uk (S. 28 (Stand: 15.06.09)); Shutterstock, New York (S. 9: Tracey Whiteside; S. 12 Bild 1: Nikolay Titov, Bild 2: Ragne Kabanova, Bild 6: Tatjana Strelkova; S. 15 London Eye: Brian A Jackson, Big Ben: Edyta Pawlowska, Buckingham Palace: Mark William Richardson, hotel: Wendy Nero; S. 18 oben re.: Felix Mizioznikov, unten li.: Gorilla, oben li.: Vale de Sousa; S. 29: Four Oaks; S. 30 oben li.: Losevsky Pavel, unten li.: Orange Line Media, unten re.: robert paul van beets; S. 47 unten Mitte: Galina Barskaya, oben li.: Julián Rovagnati, oben re.: Michael Ransburg; S. 48 li.: Martine Oger, re. u. Mitte: Monkey Business Images; S. 55 (2. v. oben): JJ pixs, 2. v. unten: Orange Line Media, unten: Robert J. Beyers II, oben: Suzane Tucker; S. 62 Ian u. Vivian: Condor 36, Jimmy u. Sue: Yuri Arcurs; S. 68: sint; S. 70: Ivan Montero Martinez)

Textquellen
S. 28: Tickets for Pitlochry Festival Theatre. Adapted from www.pitlochry.org.uk (Stand 15.06.09)
S. 43: AvH. Adapted from www.avh.montreal.qc.ac (Stand 15.06.09)
Lösungsheft S. 12: Auszug der Seiten 200, 589, 590 aus „English G 2000 Wörterbuch – Das Wörterbuch zum Lehrwerk". Herausgegeben von der Langenscheidt-Redaktion Wörterbücher und der Cornelsen-Redaktion Englisch. © 2002 Cornelsen Verlag GmbH, Berlin und Langenscheidt KG, Berlin und München.

Titelbild
Constanze Schargan, Berlin; IFA-Bilderteam, Ottobrunn (Hintergrund Union Jack: Jon Arnold Images)

Layout und technische Umsetzung
Heike Freund, Hameln

Umschlaggestaltung
Klein & Halm Grafikdesign, Berlin

www.cornelsen.de
www.EnglishG.de

1. Auflage, 3. Druck 2014

Druck: H. Heenemann, Berlin

ISBN 978-3-06-032162-9

PEFC
PEFC/04-31-1156

PEFC zertifiziert
Dieses Produkt stammt aus nachhaltig bewirtschafteten Wäldern und kontrollierten Quellen.
www.pefc.de

INHALT

DIE NÄCHSTE KLASSENARBEIT KOMMT BESTIMMT ...

Liebe Schülerin, lieber Schüler,
wer gut vorbereitet in eine Klassenarbeit geht, kann die Aufgaben in Ruhe und mit Konzentration bearbeiten und wird dann auch gute Ergebnisse erzielen. Der Klassenarbeitstrainer hilft dir dabei. Du findest zu jeder Unit zwei Klassenarbeiten, mit denen du alle Fertigkeiten (skills) trainieren kannst, die du für die Klassenarbeiten benötigst.

Unsere Tipps für ein erfolgreiches Lernen mit deinem Klassenarbeitstrainer:

Vorbereitung
Mache dir vor der Klassenarbeit rechtzeitig einen Lernplan, in dem du festlegst, was du an welchem Tag bearbeiten willst. Plane dazu genügend Zeit ein. Hole dir bei Unklarheiten Hilfe. Am Tag vor der Arbeit wiederholst du nur kurz.

Lernheft
Besorge dir ein Schreibheft. Es dient für Schreibaufgaben und zusätzliche Übungen. Schreibe schön und übersichtlich (mit Datum, Überschrift, Aufgabe und Seite). Lege auf der 1. Seite ein Inhaltsverzeichnis an. So kannst du bei Unklarheiten immer wieder nachschlagen. Es hilft dir auch, wenn du eine Aufgabe ein zweites oder drittes Mal machen möchtest.

Lösungsheft
Vergleiche deine Lösungen mit den Musterlösungen. Sieh dir dabei deine Fehler ganz genau an und überlege, was du falsch gemacht hast. Nur so kannst du daraus lernen und die Fehler in Zukunft vermeiden.
Im Lösungsheft findest du auch die Hörtexte und Lerntipps mit weiteren Übungen.

Wiederholung
Aufgaben, die dir noch schwer fallen, solltest du ein zweites oder drittes Mal machen. Lass etwas Zeit zwischen den Wiederholungen verstreichen.

Punkteschlüssel
Er hilft dir, deine Leistung einzuschätzen.

Übrigens: Die Klassenarbeiten in diesem Heft prüfen das Gelernte sehr ausführlich ab. Du brauchst daher für die Bearbeitung länger als eine Schulstunde. Natürlich kannst du dir die Klassenarbeiten auch auf einzelne Tage aufteilen oder bestimmte Aufgaben ganz gezielt üben.

Let's get started!

Ich wünsche dir viel Erfolg und vor allem viel Freude beim Üben und Lernen mit deinem Klassenarbeitstrainer.

Have fun with English!

Bärbel Schweitzer

Gesamtpunktzahl ______ / 62 Note ______

LISTENING

______ / 15

01/02 Going to London

You're on holiday in Britain and listening to Radio Rainbow. It's the afternoon programme – the reporter is talking about a quiz on last week's show and is going to announce the winner.

About the radio show

______ / 6

a) *Listen to the two texts and tick (✔) the correct box.*

	Right	Wrong
1 There was a quiz on the radio show.		
2 Last week's radio show was about planning a trip to London.		
3 You had to write a report about London to win a prize.		
4 Every listener had the right answer.		
5 The prize was a ticket for a music festival.		
6 You can win something in next week's show.		

b) *Now listen to each of the texts again for details.*

☞ Mache dir vor dem Hören bewusst, welche Einzelheiten du heraushören sollst. Lass dich nicht von anderen Einzelheiten ablenken.

01 Text 1

______ / 3

Circle the correct information.

1 Victoria Park was opened in **1845** / **1854** / **1945**.

2 Chris answered the questions **in an e-mail** / **on the phone** / **in a letter**.

3 Chris **is a student** / **is too young for a trip to London** / **is from London**.

→

02 Text 2

____ / 6

The reporter talks to Tom about ...
*Tick (✔) **Yes** or **No**.*

	Yes	No
1 ... the dinner on the first evening.		
2 ... planning the sightseeing tour.		
3 ... shopping in London.		
4 ... a boat trip on the River Thames.		
5 ... free tickets for the theatre.		
6 ... how Chris will travel to London.		

LANGUAGE

____ / 27

1 WORDS A quiz about transport

____ / 8

Fill in the correct words.

1 If you want to fly to Australia, you must go to the ______________ .
2 Your plane leaves from __________ number B34.
3 If you need a ticket for the bus, you can get it from the ticket ______________ .
4 Another word for the underground in London is the ________ .
5 Let's see which ______________ the train leaves from.
6 If you go by train and you only go one way, you need a ______________ ticket.
7 The colours on the Tube map show you the different ____________ .
8 If you put the letters from the blue boxes in the right order, you get a word that has to do with traffic:

_ _ _ _ h _ u _

2 WORDS Word groups

____ / 9

Find three more words for each word group.

Instruments	Buildings and places in town	Food

fiddle	cathedral	turkey
r ____________	s ____________	p ____________
t ____________	c ____________	b ____________
f ____________	l ____________	o ____________

3 GRAMMAR Before the weekend in London

____/5

*It's Thursday evening, the evening before Chris and his father leave for their weekend in London. Write down what Chris and his father have already done and what they haven't done. Use **already** and **not ... yet** in your sentences.*

1

Chris and his father – pack – suitcases

2

Chris's father check – train times

3

Chris – read – book about London

4

Chris's father – phone – hotel in London

5
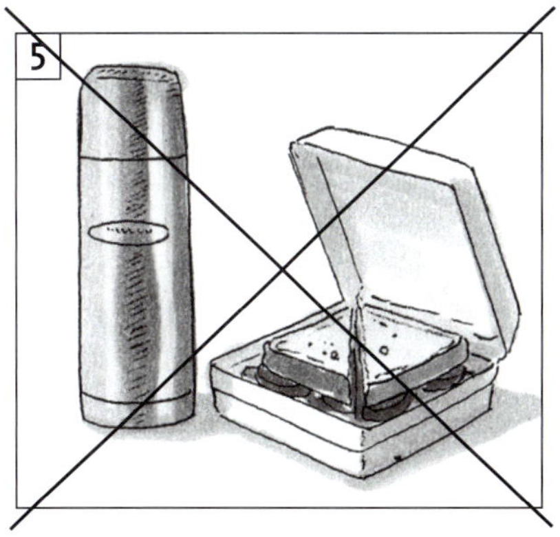

they – make – sandwiches for the train journey

1 ______________________________

2 ______________________________

3 ______________________________

4 ______________________________

5 ______________________________

present perfect

Bildung:

I/you/we/they (Lisa and Ben) **have/haven't** open**ed** the window.
he (Ben, my father) / **she** (Lisa, my daughter) / **it** (the wind) **has/hasn't** open**ed** the window.

Verwendung:

Mit dem **present perfect** drückst du aus, dass etwas irgendwann in der Vergangenheit stattgefunden hat. Der genaue Zeitpunkt des Geschehens ist nicht wichtig oder nicht bekannt. Deshalb findest du oft Adverbien der unbestimmten Zeit:

I have **already** packed my suitcase. (**already** steht vor dem past participle)
They haven**'t** read the book **yet**. (**yet** steht am Satzende)

4 GRAMMAR After the trip to London

____/5

When Tom comes back from London, he tells his mother what he and his father did, and when.
Look at Tom's notes and write ***five*** *sentences in the simple past. Always say when they did the things.*

Sat			Sun
8	*have breakfast*	*have breakfast*	8
10	*visit the London Eye*	*buy two T-shirts at Brick Lane Market*	10
12	*go on a boat trip on the River Thames*	*visit Madame Tussauds*	12
2	*look at dinosaurs in the Natural History museum*		2
4		*relax in Hyde Park*	4
6	*have dinner at a Chinese restaurant*		6

We had breakfast at 8 o'clock on Saturday and Sunday.

1 ____________________

2 ____________________

3 ____________________

4 ____________________

5 ____________________

simple past

Bildung:
Yesterday we play**ed** football. *(regelmäßig)*
We **went** to London last week. *(unregelmäßig)*

Verwendung:
Mit dem **simple past** drückst du aus, dass etwas zu einem bestimmten Zeitpunkt oder in einem bestimmten abgeschlossenen Zeitraum in der Vergangenheit geschah. (Frage: Wann?) Daher findest du in simple past-Sätzen oft genaue Zeitangaben wie *last weekend, yesterday, a week ago, in 2005, …*

WRITING

____/20

A diary about our trip to London

In her summer holidays, Sue spends four days in London with her parents and her brother.
You are Sue and write your diary about your first day.
Write down what you liked ☺ and what you didn't like ☹. Write about your feelings[1] too. Write about 100 words.

Writing better sentences:

Choose from these lists:

Linking words	**Adjectives**	**Adverbs**
Time phrases: at 7 o'clock, in the afternoon, then, next, at first, for an hour, after two hours, ... **Achtung:** Satzstellung bleibt: S-V-O: In the afternoon I played football. **Nicht:** ~~In the afternoon played I football.~~ Konjunktionen: although, and, because, but, ...	boring excited long angry happy nice spicy mild special great ...	very really ...

1 journey to London by car – too long in the car!! ☹ (4P)

2 didn't find the hotel – Mum angry with Dad – no map of London ☹ (4P)

3 hotel super – rooms very nice – everybody happy ☺ (3P)

4 afternoon: first Buckingham Palace – boring ☹ – Hyde Park – relax ☺ (5P)

5 evening: Indian restaurant – food great ☺ – now tired (4P)

Start like this:

Dear diary,

Mum, Dad, Ron and I started our journey to London this morning ...

[1] feeling ['fi:lɪŋ] *Gefühl*

Klassenarbeit B

Gesamtpunktzahl ohne Speaking ______ / 56 Note ______

Gesamtpunktzahl mit Speaking ______ / 68 Note ______

READING

______ / 15

Victoria Park

London is famous for its parks: everybody knows Hyde Park and Regent's Park. Every day many people spend some time in one of the London parks. One of London's best kept secrets[1] is another park, Victoria Park. It is in the north-east of London and it is free. It's a fantastic place to spend some free time.

Queen Victoria opened the park in 1845 because more than 30,000 people asked for a park in the part of London called the East End. Of course Hyde Park is much older, but Victoria Park was the first park in the East End. In the park people could spend some time in the fresh air, see a lot of different trees and go for a walk with their children.

In the Victorian Age[2] everybody called it the "People's Park". One of the reasons for this name was that it was a park especially for working-class[3] people. People in the Victorian Age thought that parks helped working-class people to stay healthy and to live longer. Many children visited the park every day and for some children in the 1880s it was the only place with trees and grass where they could play. People could swim in the lakes too.

Today Grove Road runs through the park and so there are two parts, a smaller western part and an eastern part. You find a lot of attractions in the park: lakes where you can paddle, some exciting playgrounds, you can play cricket and football and see deer and goats. There is something interesting for everybody in the family.

Victoria Park is also famous for open-air music festivals. Every year in August there is the *Underage Festival* in Victoria Park. This event presents some of the best reggae, rock and electronic music for young music fans. The festival is for kids from 14 to 18 only, and no adults[4] are allowed. And it's a festival without alcohol. You may only drink juice, water and other non-alcoholic drinks. BBC 1 is a partner of this festival and records the live music for their radio programmes.

[1] secret ['siːkrət] *Geheimnis* [2] Victorian Age [vɪk'tɔːriən ˌeɪdʒ] *im Zeitalter von Königin Victoria (1837–1901)*
[3] working class *Arbeiterschicht* [4] adult ['ædʌlt] *Erwachsene(r)*

1 About Victoria Park

____ / 3

Tick (✔) the three pictures that the text is about.

2 Victoria Park now and then

____ / 12

Tick (✔) the correct boxes.

Markiere in den Aussagen **Schlüsselwörter (key words)**, nach denen du im Text suchen kannst, um die gesuchte Information zu finden.

	Right	Wrong	Not in the text
1 Somebody from the Royal Family opened the park.			
2 In 1845 more than 30,000 people wanted a park in the north-east of London.			
3 Victoria Park is the oldest park in London.			
4 Another name for Victoria Park was "People's Park" because many people visited the park every day.			
5 You can still swim in the lakes in Victoria Park today.			
6 Today there is a western part and a larger eastern part.			
7 You can watch animals in Victoria Park.			
8 Victoria Park is only interesting for children.			
9 You can only visit Victoria Park during[1] the day.			
10 You are not allowed to ride your bike in the park.			
11 You are not allowed to drink alcohol at the *Underage Festival*.			
12 You can listen to some of the music from the *Underage Festival* on the radio.			

[1] during ['dʒʊərɪŋ] *während*

LANGUAGE

____ / 31

1 GRAMMAR Wednesday afternoon at Victoria Park

____ / 10

a) *Imagine it is four o'clock on Wednesday. Look at the pictures and write down what the people have already done and what they haven't done yet.*

three boys – play football

people – listen to a concert

an old lady – read a book

mother and her two children – look at the deer

man – cut the grass

two tourists – visit the park

1 ______________________________

2 ______________________________

3 ______________________________

4 ______________________________

5 ______________________________

6 ______________________________

b) *Now write* ***four*** *questions to ask the two tourists and find out what they have done in the park today. Use* ***just, yet, ever****.*

1 ______________________________

2 ______________________________

3 ______________________________

4 ______________________________

____

present perfect: questions

Have	you	**seen** the film?
What have	you	**done**?
Why have	you	**come** to this cinema?

2 GRAMMAR About two tourists

____/10

You talk to two more tourists, Ricky and Kelly, in Victoria Park, and they tell you about their sightseeing tour in London. Look at the pictures and write down what they have already done and when they did it. Use the verbs in the box:

visit • be (2x) • have dinner • take • be shopping

1

Monday morning

2

Monday afternoon

3

Tuesday afternoon

4

Tuesday afternoon

5

Tuesday evening

6

Wednesday afternoon

Start like this:

1 *Ricky and Sue have already visited the London Eye. They visited it on Monday morning.*

2 ______________________________

3 ______________________________

4 ______________________________

5 ______________________________

6 ______________________________

present perfect und **simple past** im Vergleich

Wenn du sagen möchtest, dass du etwas schon gemacht hast, der Zeitpunkt ist dabei unwichtig: **present perfect**.
I have **already** visited the London Eye.

Wenn du den genauen Zeitpunkt nennst: **simple past**.
We visited it on **Monday morning**.

3 WORDS Last week in Victoria Park

____/11

Read the sentences and fill in the missing words. Choose from the words in the box. There are three more than you need.

ending • helmet • excited • plug • surprise • shocked • flash • friendly • Tube • button • travelcards • moment • opinion • electricity

Last week there was an open-air theatre in Victoria Park. Sally and I wanted to go there. So we went by ______________________. It was good that we could use our ______________________. We were very ______________________, because it was a crime story[1]. When it started, a young man came into a room. For a ______________________ we were ______________________ because he pulled out the ______________________ so that the room was dark. Then a second man came in. He pressed a ______________________ and the light went on again. I liked him because he looked so ______________________. After the play an interviewer from a newspaper asked us about our ______________________ of the play. I told him that I liked it because the ______________________ was a big ______________________. I won't tell you the whole story! You must go and watch it yourself!

[1] crime story ['kraɪm ˌstɔːri] *Krimi*

MEDIATION

___/10

Autumn in London

Dein Onkel und deine Tante planen anlässlich ihres Hochzeitstages am 24. Oktober einen Aufenthalt in London. Dein Onkel hat im Internet ein Angebot gefunden und bittet dich um deine Hilfe.

Come to London this autumn

A three-star hotel and organized sightseeing tours are waiting for you.
Choose your trip and enjoy some wonderful days in the capital of the United Kingdom.

You organize your flight to London … we do the rest. You will stay in our comfortable three-star hotel not far from the centre of London (Tube station near the hotel). Rooms include TV, telephone and private bathroom. Every day we will show you some wonderful sights in London. Is there a special reason why you are coming to London? Just tell us and we will have a surprise present waiting for you.

YOU CAN VISIT LONDON FOR THREE OR FOUR DAYS AND CHOOSE FROM THESE DATES: 2nd OCT, 14th OCT, 23rd OCT, 27th OCT		
DATE	THREE NIGHTS	FOUR NIGHTS
2nd OCT	*£155	£198
14th OCT	£150	£190
23rd OCT	£145	£185
27th OCT	£140	£180

*We serve you a special candlelit[1] dinner on the second evening of your visit.

Prices are for one person and include:

- three/four nights with breakfast and dinner in the hotel's restaurant and
- the following interesting sightseeing programmes:
  three nights: two half-day and one full-day sightseeing programme
  four nights: two half-day and two full-day sightseeing programmes
- If you are interested, we will organize the tickets for your evening activities (theatre, musical, cinema, …) and organize your transport. Or just spend the evening in our nice hotel bar.

Interested? Then what are you waiting for?
Do you want to find out more about our hotel and our sightseeing tours?

Fill in this form.

Name:

Address:

Telephone number:

E-mail:

All the information will be in your mailbox in no more than three days.

[1] candlelit dinner ['kændllɪt] *romantisches Abendessen bei Kerzenschein*

Dein Onkel Ich habe hier ein Angebot in London gefunden. Es scheint sich um ein 3-Sterne-Hotel zu handeln. Aber viel mehr verstehe ich nicht. Ist ein Flug dabei und was steht da über die Hotelzimmer? (2P)

Du ______________________________

____

Dein Onkel Wie sieht es mit der Verpflegung aus – welche anderen Mahlzeiten gibt es außer dem Frühstück? (1P)

Du ______________________________

Dein Onkel Sie schreiben etwas über Aktivitäten am Abend. Gibt es auch ein organisiertes Abendprogramm? (3P)

Du ______________________________

____

Dein Onkel Jetzt mal zu den Preisen. Ich sehe, dass es unterschiedliche Preise für drei oder vier Nächte gibt, das ist klar. Aber was bieten sie eigentlich zusätzlich an, wenn man vier Nächte bleibt? (1P)

Du ______________________________

Dein Onkel Und was bedeutet das Sternchen? (1P)

Du ______________________________

____

Dein Onkel Wo findet man etwas über das Besichtigungsprogramm? (2P)

Du ______________________________

____

____

SPEAKING

____/12

03 Talking to Dad

Josephine is a British girl. She is 14 years old and lives in a village not far from London.
Last week she went shopping in London with her friends.
When she came home, her father wanted to know everything.

Höre dir Josephines Antworten genau an und mache dir Notizen.
Sie helfen dir, wenn du in **Now you** Josephines Rolle übernimmst.

04 Now you

This time Josephine went to the Underage Festival in Victoria Park in London.
She is talking to her father. Again he wants to know everything. Take Josephine's part.

Before you start, think about the following things and make notes about ...

- who you went with
- how you got to London
- how you found your way to Victoria Park
- which line you took to Victoria Park (Tube station: Bethnal Green / ... line / ... bound)
- how much you paid for the entrance ticket for the *Underage Festival* (free)
- some details about the *Underage Festival* (bands, drinks, the kids' ages ...)
- when you got home – "no more questions"

Du kannst nochmals den Text „Victoria Park" auf S. 10 lesen. Dort findest du einige Informationen über das *Underage Festival*, die dir für diese Unterhaltung nützlich sein können.
Orientiere dich auch auf dem U-Bahn-Plan auf S. 14 in deinem Englischbuch.

Klassenarbeit A

Gesamtpunktzahl ______ / 70 Note ______

READING

____ / 17

☞ Verschaffe dir zuerst einen Überblick, um was es in dem Text geht: Überschrift, Bilder, Text einmal lesen (**skimming**).
Lies dir dann die Aufgaben zum Text durch und suche nun anhand von Schlüsselwörtern gezielt nach den gefragten Informationen (**scanning**).

SCOTMAG – *your magazine for Scotland*

Going to school in Scotland

Dear readers,

In the coming weeks we want to tell you more about how students get to school. This week we are having a look at our students from Scotland. Many of our Scottish students go to school by bus or bike, but there are others …

Take Alice, 13, from the Isle of Flotta. She goes to school by ferry and bus – quite exciting, isn't it? It takes her about one and a half hours every Monday morning. That's why Alice stays at the school hostel during the week until she goes home again on Friday afternoon. Alice: "I miss my family a lot."

Going to school is a lot easier and quicker for Leo, 16, from Aberdeen. Leo's father is a taxi driver. He takes Leo to school every morning before he starts working. Leo likes it because he needn't get up so early. Leo: "It only takes me seven minutes to get to school, but sometimes I would like to spend some time before school on the bus together with my classmates."

Joel, 13, from Glasgow likes sleeping long – and he can sleep long every morning, because he lives right next to the school. Joel: "If I had a long journey to school, I would ask my parents to move nearer to the school. I hate getting up early."

Janet, 14, lives just outside Edinburgh and goes to school by train. She likes trains, stations and the different people at the stations. It takes her about half an hour to get to her school. Janet: "I enjoy my journey to school – I can read magazines and I have time to learn my German and French vocabulary."

Find out about Robert's funny way of going to school in next week's "SCOTMAG". We are interested in getting more information from Scottish students and from students from other parts of Britain or even from students from other countries. Just tell us how you get to school, how long it takes you, if you like it or if you don't, and why. Please contact us by e-mail.

1 About going to school

___ / 6

Look at the pictures. Read the text and tick (✔) the ***six*** *things or situations that the text is about.*

2 The shortest journey to school

___ / 4

Write down numbers 1, 2, 3 and 4 next to the names below:
1 for the shortest and 4 for the longest time to go to school.

Alice ____________

Leo ____________

Joel ____________

Janet ____________

3 More about the article

___ / 7

Read the text again and find out if these sentences are right, wrong or not in the text.

	Right	Wrong	Not in the text
1 Every morning Alice goes to school by ferry.			
2 Leo misses his friends in the morning.			
3 Leo's father picks him up after school.			
4 Joel is quite happy with his journey to school.			
5 Janet likes going by train.			
6 The four students like school a lot.			
7 The magazine is looking for information from students in other countries too.			

LANGUAGE

____ / 25

1 WORDS John Bennet, Isle of Flotta

____ / 13

a) *Fill in the missing words. They are all new in this unit.*
Be careful: in the box there are two more words than you need. (9P)

imagine • arrival • great-grandmother • upset • lonely once • salmon • departure • post • timetable • farmer

John Bennet lives on the Isle of Flotta. He is a ____________ and works on a ____________ farm. When he is out with the boat, his wife and his daughter Alice often feel ____________. ____________ a month the family visits Alice's ____________, Bennet in Kirkwall on Mainland. They must take the ferry to Mainland. The ____________ of the ferry is early in the morning. As you can ____________, Glenna Bennet always waits for the ____________ of her family. Sometimes John and his family can't visit Glenna – then she is very ____________.

b) *Explain the following two words in a complete sentence (4P):*

great-grandmother: ____________

____

timetable: ____________

____

2 WORDS Find the words.

____ / 6

Find the words and fill them in.

1 I have invited six guests to my party – I _ _ _ _ _ ☐ six guests.

2 Joe is a good friend – he is a good _ ☐ _ _.

3 If you can't talk to a person on your mobile, you can send a ☐ _ _ _ _ _ ☐ _ ☐ _ _.

4 If you have learned your new words, you know their _ _ _ ☐ ☐ _ _.

5 Tonight I want to write in my diary – I want to make an _ ☐ _ ☐ _.

6 If you put the letters in the boxes from 1–5 in the right order, you get a word for an exercise that you sometimes do in your English lesson: ☐ ☐ ☐ ☐ ☐ l ☐ ☐ ☐ o ☐

3 GRAMMAR What would happen if …

_____ / 6

Complete the sentences. The following ideas in the box will help you.

be very unhappy • forget to learn it at home • sleep longer on Mondays
father not have a taxi • miss the train to Edinburgh • ????

1 If Alice lived in Kirkwall, ______________________________.

2 Leo would go by bus ______________________________.

3 If Joel's parents moved to another part of the town, ______________________________.

4 Janet could learn her German vocabulary on the train ______________________________.

5 Janet would be late ______________________________.

6 If I lived on the Isle of Hoy, ______________________________.

if-Sätze Typ 2 – „Was wäre, wenn …"
Mit if-Sätzen Typ 2 kannst du ausdrücken, was unter bestimmten Bedingungen sein könnte, aber doch eher unwahrscheinlich ist (oder sogar unmöglich).

if-Satz (Bedingung)	Hauptsatz (Folge)
If I **won** a million euros,	I **would/could buy** a nice house for my family.
simple past	*would/could + infinitive*

STUDY SKILLS

_____ / 8

USING A DICTIONARY More information about Joel

You have to translate a few German sentences into English, but you don't know all the words. Use a dictionary and find the correct English words for the underlined German words.

Lies immer erst den gesamten Wörterbucheintrag, bevor du dich für eine bestimmte Übersetzung entscheidest. Oft werden weitere Informationen gegeben, die du brauchst, um die richtige Übersetzung zu finden.

1 Joel interessiert sich für den <u>Weltraum</u>. (1P)

Joel is interested in ____________________.

2 Er liest viele Bücher über dieses <u>Thema</u> und <u>sucht</u> <u>Informationen</u> <u>im Internet</u>. (4P)

He reads many books on this ____________________ and ____________________

____________________ ____________________.

3 Letzte Woche <u>hielt</u> er <u>sogar</u> einen <u>Vortrag</u> darüber. (3P)

Last week he ____________________ ____________________ ____________________ about it.

WRITING

___/20

An e-mail to SCOTMAG

On the internet you read the article in SCOTMAG about going to school.
Now you want to write a comment[1] and tell them about how you get to school.

- Beginne deine E-Mail mit einem interessanten Satz.
- Schreibe am Anfang, um was es in deiner E-Mail geht.
- Fange für jeden neuen Gedanken einen neuen Abschnitt an.
  (Jeder Spiegelstrich – siehe unten – entspricht einem neuen Abschnitt.)
- Beende deine E-Mail mit einem abschließenden Satz oder einer Frage an den Adressaten.

Write about the following things:

– what you think about the article "Going to school", and say why you think so

– who you are and where you live in Germany

– when you get up, how you get to school, how long it takes

– why you like / don't like your journey to school

– what you will tell your friends about the article

Start your e-mail like this:

Dear SCOTMAG,

[1] comment ['kɒment] *Kommentar*

Gesamtpunktzahl ohne Speaking	______ / 58	Note ______
Gesamtpunktzahl mit Speaking	______ / 75	Note ______

LISTENING

______ / 17

05 A presentation about Pitlochry, Scotland

Today Rick, one of Katrina's classmates, gives a presentation about Pitlochry, a small country town in Scotland. Listen to his presentation.

New word
ladder ['lædə] *Leiter*

1 The presentation

______ / 5

Look at the pictures. Listen to the text and put the pictures into the right order. Be careful: there are two more pictures than you need.

A
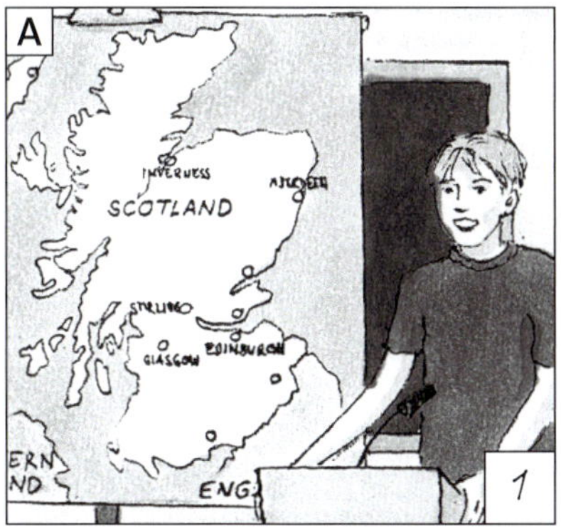

B

C

D

E

F
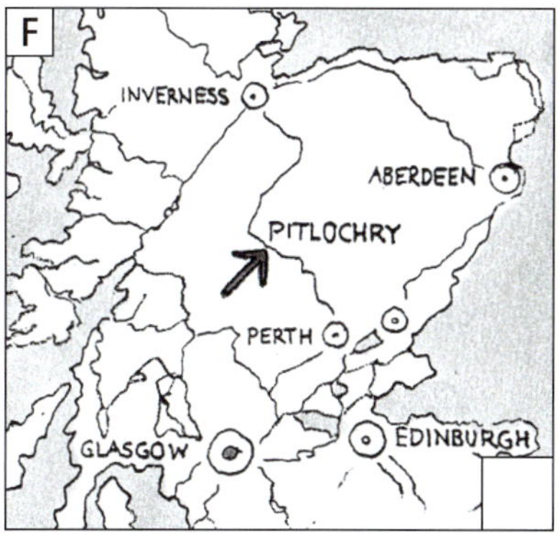

G

H

2 Come and spend your holidays in Pitlochry

_____ / 8

Listen again. Match the sentence halves and draw lines.
Be careful: there are three more endings than you need.

1 Pitlochry is
2 Pitlochry looks
3 Many people come
4 You can explore the Highlands
5 Come and see
6 The Pitlochry Highland Games
7 If you come to Pitlochry,
8 People from all over the world

a) our famous salmon ladder!
b) if you are staying in Pitlochry.
c) to visit Pitlochry every year.
d) come to the Festival Theatre.
e) you will meet people from all over the world.
f) in the heart of Scotland.
g) a bit like 100 years ago.
h) to stay in caravans.
i) are an attraction for old and young people.
j) if you want to go snowboarding.
k) you will dance a lot.

3 Information about Pitlochry

_____ / 4

Listen to the text again. Tick (✔) the right box.

1 At the beginning of his presentation Rick gives information about	the number of hotels in Pitlochry.	☐
	the structure of his presentation.	☐
	the youth hostel in Pitlochry.	☐

2 In Pitlochry	there are stone houses.	☐
	there are 2,800 people.	☐
	there are 3,500 people.	☐

3 Visitors to Pitlochry	can stay in a caravan.	☐
	never stay at hotels.	☐
	can stay at a Bed and Breakfast.	☐

4 If you visit the Pitlochry Highland Games,	you can watch Scottish sports.	☐
	you need an entrance ticket.	☐
	you will come in August.	☐

LANGUAGE

____/29

1 WORDS Just the opposite

____/5

Find the opposites:

1 remember ◂▸ ______________________ 4 small ◂▸ ______________________

2 arrival ◂▸ ______________________ 5 begin ◂▸ ______________________

3 above ◂▸ ______________________

2 WORDS In town

____/12

a) *Look at the picture and complete the list with the things that you can see. Add* ***four*** *more words. (9P)*

buildings, places	traffic
extra:	extra:

b) *Complete the sentences about the following places. Write what you can do there. (3P)*

At the station you can ____

At the post office you ____

At the cinema you ____

3 GRAMMAR Jason from Pitlochry

_____/4

Jason thinks about what would happen if … Complete his sentences.

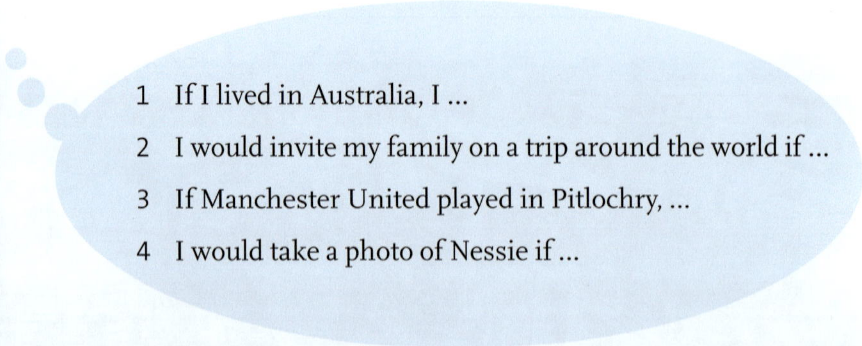

1 If I lived in Australia, ____.

2 I would invite my family on a trip around the world ____.

3 If Manchester United played in Pitlochry, ____.

4 I would take a photo of Nessie ____.

☞ **If-Sätze Typ 2 – „Was wäre, wenn …“**
Mit if-Sätzen Typ zwei kannst du ausdrücken, was unter bestimmten Bedingungen sein könnte, aber doch eher unwahrscheinlich ist (oder sogar unmöglich).

if-Satz (Bedingung)	**Hauptsatz (Folge)**
If I **won** a million euros,	I **would/could buy** a nice house for my family.
simple past	*would/could + infinitive*

4 WORDS Last year in Pitlochry

_____ /8

a) *Jacques from France is talking about his holiday camp in Pitlochry last year. Make sentences with* ***be able to*** *and* ***be allowed to****. Use the phrases from the box. (4P)*

spend three weeks in Pitlochry • go to a Scottish school • watch a good film at the cinema • listen to the best bagpipe groups

1 Last year I ____

because I had saved a lot of money.

2 With our holiday group we went to the Highland Games and there we

____.

3 When I stayed at the holiday camp last year, one day I

____.

4 One evening my friends and I

____.

Now you

b) *Write four sentences and say what you will able to do / you will be allowed to do next year. Here are some ideas: (4P)*

Next year I will be allowed to go on holiday without my parents.

Next year I will be able to spend some time in England.

1 ____

2 ____

3 ____

4 ____

☞ be able to do sth. = etwas tun können; fähig sein / in der Lage sein, etwas zu tun
be allowed to do sth. = etwas tun dürfen

Um diese Ausdrücke an die jeweilige Zeitform anzupassen, muss nur „be“ verändert werden:
I **am** allowed to ... / I **was** allowed to ... / they **were** allowed to ... / I **will be** allowed to ...

MEDIATION

___/12

Tickets for Pitlochry Festival Theatre

PITLOCHRY Festival Theatre | BUY ONLINE | WHAT'S ON | ACTIVE ARTS | TASTE | HIPER | VISITOR INFO | FRIENDS | HISTORY | HIRE | NEWS | CONTACT | VISIT EXPLORERS GARDEN

Buy Online

Steps to booking tickets online:

1. Click on the month you would like to come.
2. When you find the event you want, click 'Buy tickets'.
3. Next, choose the price and enter the number of tickets you want to buy.
4. Click 'Continue'.
5. Next you'll see a list of the tickets you have bought. Click 'Continue' if you are happy with your list or go back to 'Change' if not. Please note that you automatically get the best seats that are free – you cannot book special seats. This is something we hope to be able to offer in the future.
6. The next step is to enter your own personal details and the way you want to pay.
7. Click 'Buy tickets'.

DISCOVER ... TASTE ... HEAR ... TRY ... CREATE ... SEE ... DISCOVER ... TASTE ... HEAR ... TRY ... CREATE ... SEE ...

Your family is planning a trip to Scotland. You help your mother with the tickets for the Pitlochry Festival Theatre.

Deine Mutter Ich habe jetzt die Veranstaltung angeklickt, für die ich Karten kaufen will. Und was mache ich jetzt?

Du ______________________________

______________________________ (3P)

Deine Mutter Ah, jetzt sehe ich eine Liste mit den Karten. Aber Mensch, ich hab ja die falschen angeklickt! Kann ich das nochmal rückgängig machen?

Du ______________________________

______________________________ (2P)

Deine Mutter Gut, nochmal von vorne ... Ja, das sind jetzt die richtigen Karten. Jetzt möchte ich mir gerne noch Plätze aussuchen. Wie mache ich das?

Du ______________________________

______________________________ (3P)

Deine Mutter Und wie gehts jetzt weiter?

Du ______________________________

______________________________ (4P)

SPEAKING

____/17

06 Booking tickets on the phone

Mrs Baker is phoning the Pitlochry Festival Theatre booking office. Listen to the dialogue.

Höre dir Mrs Bakers Antworten genau an und sprich sie nach. Mache dir Notizen. Sie helfen dir, wenn du im **Now you** selbst ein Telefongespräch führst.

07 Now you

You are staying with your penfriend Sue in Scotland. You want to go to one of the plays at Pitlochry Festival Theatre. Look at the programme and choose one of the plays. Then ring up the booking office and talk to the lady at the office.

	November		December		January		February		March
3	*Hot Chili Pepper*	1	*Sally and Joe*	6	*Sally and Joe*	2	*The Scottish Dream*	1	*A Bad Mistake*
12	*Ghosts*	2	*An Invitation*	10	*Ghosts*	8	*Hot Chili Pepper*	14	*An Invitation*
17	*Black and White*	15	*Hot Chili Pepper*	14	*Sally and Joe*	12	*An Invitation*	15	*Black and White*
25	*Hot Chili Pepper*	20	*Sally and Joe*	26	*The Scottish Dream*	20	*The Scottish Dream*	18	*An Invitation*
27	*Ghosts*	25	*Hot Chili Pepper*	27	*Ghosts*	22	*Hot Chili Pepper*	27	*A Bad Mistake*
30	*Black and White*	31	*An Invitation*	29	*The Scottish Dream*	27	*An invitation*	30	*Black and White*

Falls du dir zum Buchstabieren deines Namens das englische Alphabet in Erinnerung rufen willst, findest du es in deinem Englischbuch auf S. 229.

Klassenarbeit A

Gesamtpunktzahl ohne Speaking _____ / 70	Note _____
Gesamtpunktzahl mit Speaking _____ / 90	Note _____

READING

_____ / 11

Die erste Aufgabe zum Lesetext auf S. 31 hilft dir, einen ersten Überblick zu bekommen, um was es in der Broschüre geht. Lies also zuerst Aufgabe 1 und überfliege dann den Text anhand der Überschriften, der Bilder und des ersten Satzes jedes Abschnitts.

Sports and English – teenage holiday camps

About us

We are a great team of young people who organize two-week summer camps in Germany.

We want young people from all over Germany to have fun with English, enjoy all kinds of sports and spend two weeks outdoors. This year camps will be in Freiburg, Rostock, Munich and Dresden.

English is fun

The language in the camps is English so you have the chance to speak English all day. From Monday to Friday there are also special English courses every morning (90 minutes). There are only six to ten students in one group.

Don't expect boring school lessons! No, we want you to have fun with English. We listen to the English radio news, watch English films, read the newspaper. We talk, discuss and ... sing. All our teachers are native speakers[1] who help you to make the most of your abilities. All our teachers also speak German fluently.

Sport is fun

There are lots of activities that you can choose from. During the first two days of your stay we will show you all kinds of sports – football, tennis, baseball, table tennis, surfing*, swimming, hockey, volleyball and aerobics. On the third day you tell us what you are going to concentrate on: you choose one main sport activity. You can add one or two activities that you would like to get to know better.

* Please note that surfing is only possible in the Rostock camp.

Daily life is fun

You will sleep in tents and we will cook our own meals together. We want to be good sportspeople so alcohol, cigarettes and drugs[2] are not allowed in the camp.

- **Last year more than 800 teenagers between 12 and 17 from all over Germany came to our camps.**
- **Come and join one of our camps this year!**
- **Find out more and visit our website: www.sports&english.com**

SPECIAL OFFER €490

[1] native speaker [ˌneɪtɪv ˈspiːkə] *Muttersprachler/in*   [2] drugs [drʌgz] *Drogen*

1 What is the brochure about?

____ / 1

Tick (✔) the right statement.

The brochure is about ...

... teenagers in a British summer camp.	
... learning English in an outdoor summer camp.	
... summer camps where you do lots of sport activities and learn English.	
... how sporty students spend their summer holidays in England.	

2 Susanna is interested in the camp

____ / 10

Susanna from Freiburg has read the brochure. Now she is telling her English teacher at school all about it. Complete her sentences with information from the text.

1 The camps are in ____________________.

2 The teenagers come from ____________________.

3 They sleep ____________________.

4 In the camp you are not allowed to ____________________.

5 You learn English in ____________________.

6 In the English courses they ____________________

____________________. *(Write two facts.)*

7 The teachers speak ____________________.

8 After the second day you ____________________.

9 You can go surfing in ____________________.

☞ **Sätze vervollständigen (Completing sentences)**
Bei dieser Aufgabenform musst du auf zwei Dinge achten: auf den Inhalt **und** auf die grammatikalische Korrektheit. Das bedeutet, dass du den vorgegebenen Satzanfang so ergänzen musst, dass sich ein vollständiger, richtiger Satz ergibt.

LANGUAGE

____/29

1 WORDS Camp activity: football

____/10

Collect words that are linked with football and add them to this mind map. Find at least ***ten*** *words.*

Du kannst in dieser Mindmap selbstständig weitere Äste ergänzen.

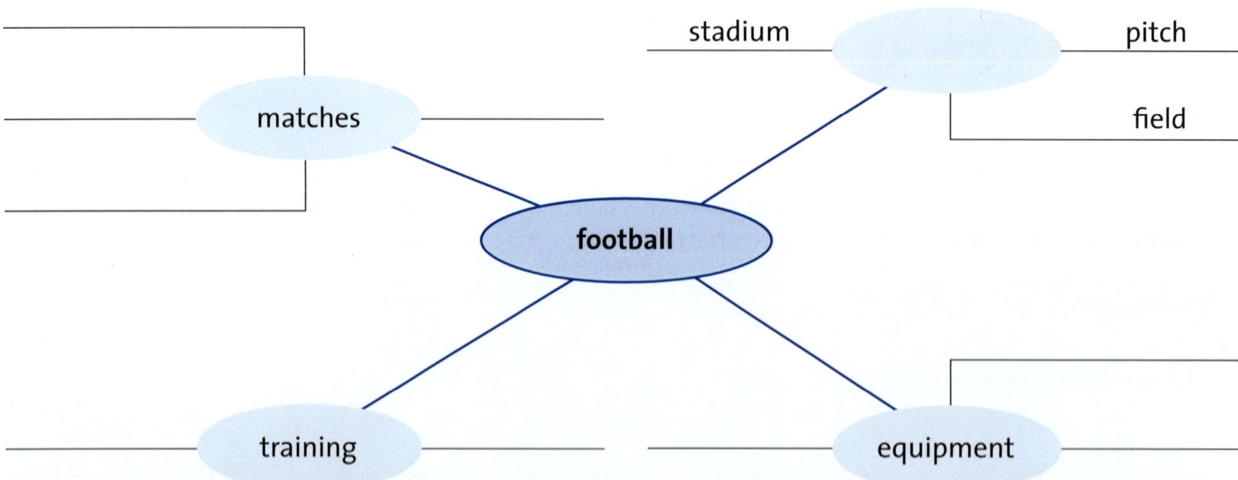

2 WORDS More sports

____/10

a) *What four sports can you see in the pictures?*
Write down the equipment that you need too and where you do each sport. (6P)

sport	equipment	location

b) *Choose* ***two*** *sports. Write two sentences about each sport. Write where you do it and what you need. (4P)*

Example:

You play table tennis in a sports hall. You need a table tennis bat.

1 ______________________________

2 ______________________________

3 GRAMMAR Susanna and the camp

___/9

a) *Write sentences. Use **who** or **that**. (5P)*

1 Susanna / student / comes from Freiburg

2 Susanna / the only student / came to the camp by bus

3 Tennis and football / the two activities / Susanna chose on the third day

4 Aerobics / a sport / many girls in the camp chose as their favourite activity

5 Mike / English teacher / always starts the lesson with a song

6 Nate / only boy / chose aerobics

Example:

1 *Susanna is a student who comes from Freiburg.*

2 ______________________________

3 ______________________________

4 ______________________________

5 ______________________________

6 ______________________________

b) *Finish these sentences and use **who** or **that**. (2P)*

1 Frank is a student ______________________________.

2 Basketball is a sport ______________________________.

„who" oder **„that"**?

who in Relativsätzen, die **Personen** beschreiben:
The **girl who** plays football well is called Nina.

that in Relativsätzen, die **Dinge** (und namenlose Tiere) beschreiben.
The **book that** I read was a present from my sister.

c) *There are two sentences in **a)** where you don't need **who** or **that**. Which are they? (2P)*

☐ ☐

STUDY SKILLS

___ / 15

PARAPHRASING Susanna is getting by in English

a) *When Susanna speaks English, she sometimes doesn't know the correct English words. So she paraphrases them. (12P)*

Wenn du ein Wort umschreiben möchtest, kannst du so anfangen:
- It's something that ...
- It's a place where ...
- It's somebody who ...

1 Trainer

______________________________.

2 Friseur

______________________________.

3 Gemeindehalle

______________________________.

4 Durchsage

______________________________.

5 Helm

______________________________.

6 Bahnsteig

______________________________.

b) *Now tell Susanna the correct English words. (3P)*

1 ______________ 4 ______________

2 ______________ 5 ______________

3 ______________ 6 ______________

MEDIATION

____/15

Summer camp scholarship[1] – information for parents

Dear parents,
Once again there are scholarships that families with three or more children can ask for. There is a total amount[2] of €5000 that we will give those families who have asked for scholarships. So it is important that you apply[3] for the scholarship early in the year. Please understand that you can only apply for one scholarship even if more than one of your children wants to join our camps.

What you should do

- ★ You may apply for not more than €200.
- ★ Tell us the amount of money you are asking for.
- ★ Apply before 1 May.
- ★ Tell us your name, address, the number of children in your family and the name and date of the camp.
- ★ Tell us the amount of money your family can spend every month.
- ★ Your son or daughter should write a short essay on why he or she wants to join one of our camps.
- ★ Send everything to our office in Hamburg.
- ★ Wait for our answer.

What you should know

- ★ After you have applied for the scholarship please don't call our organization. Please wait for more information. Although we try to answer letters quickly, sometimes it takes three or four weeks.
- ★ If your family got a scholarship last year, the earliest date for another scholarship is next year. Sorry!
- ★ You can be sure that nobody in the camp will know that your family got a scholarship.

Your kids will spend two unforgettable weeks in one of our camps – so what are you waiting for?

Yours sincerely,

Pete Wyatt
Director of Scholarship for Camps

[1] scholarship *Stipendium (= finanzielle Unterstützung für Schüler/innen)* [2] amount *Betrag* [3] to apply for *sich bewerben um*

You want to go to a summer camp. Today you are talking to your parents and explain how you can apply for a scholarship.

Papa Wer kann sich überhaupt um eine solche Unterstützung bewerben?

Du ______________________________ (2P)

Mama Wie viel Geld steht insgesamt zur Verfügung und wie viel könnten wir als Familie bekommen?

Du ______________________________ (2P)

Papa Welche Angaben muss man bei der Bewerbung machen?

Du ______________________________

____

______________________________ (2P)

Mama Muss man der Bewerbung sonst noch etwas beilegen?

Du ______________________________ (2P)

Papa Wann müssen wir uns bewerben?

Du ______________________________ (1P)

Mama Und wie geht es dann weiter?

Du ______________________________ (2P)

Papa Kann man da jedes Jahr einen neuen Antrag stellen?

Du ______________________________ (2P)

Papa Gibt es sonst noch etwas Wichtiges, was wir wissen sollten?

Du ______________________________ (2P)

SPEAKING

____/20

08 Getting to know the other teenagers at the camp

In the afternoon of the first day all the teenagers at the camp in Rostock meet.
First they talk in pairs, take notes and then everybody introduces[1] another teenager to the group.
Listen to Matthias, who introduces Valentin.

Höre dir Matthias' Vorstellung an und sprich sie abschnittsweise nach.
Notiere dir hilfreiche Formulierungen für deine eigene Vorstellung im **Now you**.

Now you

Imagine you are at a camp too. Now you introduce another teenager. Invent[2] a name and other personal details. Use this notepad and make some notes before you speak.

Name ____________________

Age ____________________

Where from ____________________

- ***town/city/village*** ____________________
- ***where in Germany*** ____________________

Brothers or sisters ____________________

School ____________________

- ***languages*** ____________________
- ***favourite subject*** ____________________
- ***...*** ____________________

What he/she wants to be ____________________
(Schlage in einem Wörterbuch einen Beruf nach.) ____________________

Why here at the camp ____________________

Favourite sport ____________________

Sport he/she wants to do at the camp + why ____________________

____

[1] (to) introduce sb. [ˌɪntrəˈdjuːs] *jn. vorstellen* [2] (to) invent sth. [ɪnˈvent] *etwas erfinden*

Klassenarbeit B

Gesamtpunktzahl ______ / 52   Note ______

LISTENING

______ / 11

9 A visit to the Lowry

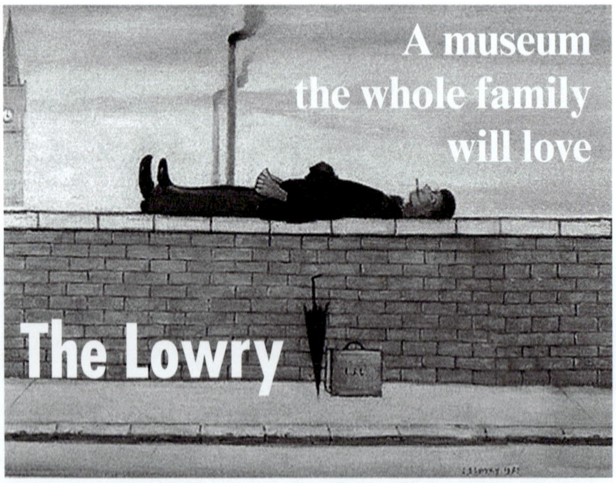

There is an advert[1] on the radio about the Lowry. Listen to it.

New words
painting ['peɪntɪŋ] *Gemälde*
puzzle ['pʌzl] *Rätsel*

Die erste Aufgabe zum Hörverstehenstext hilft dir, einen ersten Überblick zu bekommen, um was es in dem Werbespot geht. Lies die Aufgabe also vor dem ersten Hören, damit du sie dann leicht lösen kannst.

1 About the advert

______ / 1

Listen to the advert and then tick (✔) the right statement.

The advert is about ...

... the address of the Lowry.	
... the painter Lowry.	
... going to the Lowry with the whole family.	
... the times when you can visit the Lowry.	

[1] advert ['ædvɜːt] *Werbespot*

2 About the Lowry

___/5

Tick (✔) the right statement.

The Lowry is	only open for families.	☐
	a good place for families.	☐
	only for small children.	☐

The rucksacks	are a great help for families.	☐
	are not allowed in the museum.	☐
	are good for food and drinks.	☐

Next month there will be	a drama workshop.	☐
	activities for telling stories.	☐
	postcards with Lowry's paintings.	☐

In December	there are no workshops.	☐
	families don't pay to visit the museum.	☐
	Sundays are free for families.	☐

In the Lowry	you can go to the restaurant.	☐
	you can buy postcards.	☐
	you must have a rucksack.	☐

3 At home

___/5

Listen to the advert again. Sabrina has visited the Lowry.
Now she is at home again and her friend asks her questions about the Lowry.
Answer the questions. You can write short answers – you needn't write complete sentences.

1 Families can get rucksacks in the Lowry. What is in the rucksacks? *(Write two things.)*

____

2 There are two different workshops in the Lowry this month. What can you do there? *(Write two facts.)*

____

3 What is special about the "Free Family Sunday"?

____

STUDY SKILLS

____/6

PARAPHRASING Talking about the Lowry

An expert from the Lowry talks about the museum. Choose three of the words and explain them.

artist • "Free Family Sunday" • the Lowry • creative workshops • story-telling workshop

- So kannst du deine Erklärungen beginnen:
  - – ... is something
  - – ... is a person/somebody
  - – ... is a place/room
  - – ... is a day
- Wenn du für deine Worterklärung Informationen benötigst, findest du sie im abgedruckten Hörtext auf S. 24 im Lösungsheft.

1 ____________________ (2P)

2 ____________________ (2P)

3 ____________________ (2P)

LANGUAGE

____/15

1 GRAMMAR More information about the Lowry

____/8

a) *Who likes what best? Write sentences and use* ***who*** *or* ***that****. (5P)*

Um vollständige Sätze zu bilden, musst du auch noch die Verben in der richtigen Form ergänzen.

1 Children under 10 / visitors / like the story-telling workshop best

____

2 The rucksacks / an attraction / most families like

____

3 Mr L. S. Lowry / a painter / was born in Manchester

____

4 Every month / new workshops / you can join

____

5 The drama workshops / workshops / women between 25 and 45 years like best

____

b) *Read your sentences again. Write down the numbers of the sentences where you can leave out* ***who*** *or* ***that****. (3P)*

☐ ☐ ☐

2 WORDS Find the words

___/7

Find the words and fill them in.

1 Put the letters in the correct _ _ _ [ ] _ .

2 I've had these flowers since last year – they are _ _ [ ] _ _ _ [ ] _ _ _ .

3 Peggy had an accident with her bike – we had to call the _ _ _ _ _ [ ] _ _ _ .

4 She had an _ _ _ _ _ [ ] _ _ _ on her knee.

5 Larry is a good _ _ [ ] [ ] _ _ _ _ _ _ _ _ .

6 This summer our team won the _ [ ] _ _ _ [ ] _ _ [ ] _ _ _ .

Can you make a word out of the letters in the boxes from 1–6? Sentence 7 will help you.

7 I love sports like running and jumping – I love [ ] [ ] [ ] [ ] [ ] [ ] [ ] [ ] [ ] .

WRITING

____ / 20

A day out to the Lowry

Imagine you are a student at a school in Leeds. Yesterday you went on a day out to the Lowry in Manchester. You write a report about your visit to the Lowry for the school magazine.

- Denke dir eine interessante Überschrift aus.
- Schreibe am Anfang, um was es in deinem Bericht geht. Die Details kommen später.
- Mache an geeigneten Stellen einen Abschnitt.
- Beende deinen Bericht mit einem abschließenden Satz.
- Denke daran, das **simple past** zu verwenden.

In your report answer these questions:

– Who?	students of Form 7 LM
– What event was it?	a day out
– Where?	to the Lowry in Manchester – building amazing
– When?	February 25th, from 10 am – 2 pm
– Why?	do a presentation about the famous painter L. S. Lowry, find out about him, collect information, copy one of Lowry's paintings
– How?	very interesting, different games and activities around the paintings, some students: design their own postcards

Gesamtpunktzahl ______ / 69 Note ______

READING

______ / 13

http://www.avh.montreal.qc.ca

avh

Alexander von Humboldt (AvH)
German International School Montreal

Alexander von Humboldt German International School is a private school in Montreal, Canada. We have a large science and arts program[1] for all children from kindergarten to high school[2]. Many of our students have German parents or grandparents and so speak some German at home. However, not all our students have a German background – of course our school welcomes students of all nationalities. We also welcome guest students from Europe in year 10.

Children who don't speak German are welcome at our kindergarten. There they can learn the German language easily from other German-speaking children and of course from our language program. The kindergarten is open three days a week for the children from the age of 2½ to 3½, and five days a week for the children from 3½ to 5.

Languages are very important at Alexander von Humboldt School. So our teachers at AvH do not only teach three languages, they teach **in** three languages: German, French and English. This helps every student to speak the three languages very well. While German plays an important role in the first years, English and French become more important in the higher years. After year 11 students can take the Canadian High School Diploma. In year 12 students will have the chance to take the German International Abitur.

The school was opened in 1980. Today 310 students from many different countries are learning in a friendly atmosphere. Lessons can be in the classroom, but very often outside the classroom too. The little ones have sleepovers in the school, for example a book night. There are 3 full-day field trips in the country, ski trips and visits to museums, music and theatre concerts for the older students. Of course, students go abroad during their time at Alexander von Humboldt International School. There is a study trip to Germany for up to 11 days in year 8. In year 9, students can go on a study trip to New York City for four days.

Parents are an important part of our school – we want parents to play an active role and help their children make the best out of their time at Alexander von Humboldt.

Interested? Then come to our

OPEN HOUSE
October 17 and January 16
9 am – 4 pm.

We have two Open Houses a year, in October and January. Have a walk round our school and see the building with its classrooms, science and art rooms and the library. Watch our students working with our modern computers. Visit the cafeteria and you'll meet teachers, students and parents.

Come and get to know our excellent school. We will be happy to meet you at AvH.

[1] program = *amerikanische Schreibweise für* programme [2] high school ['haɪ skuːl] *(USA, Kanada) Schule für 14–18-Jährige*

1 What is the website about?

___ / 1

What is this website about? Read it and tick (✔) the correct statement. Only one answer is correct.

This website tells you about ...

... how you can find online friends at a Canadian school.	
... how German and Canadian schools work together.	
... what the school offers[1] to students.	
... how parents and students prepare the Open House.	

2 About AvH

___ / 6

Match these headings to the paragraphs 1–6. Find the best headings.
Be careful: there are three headings that you don't need.

A Activities for the students
B AvH's history
C Calendar and events
D Find out more about our school
E International contacts
F Learn different languages
G Parents support their children
H Start with German
I The students' nationalities[2]

1		2		3		4		5		6	

3 More details about AvH

___ / 6

Anwer the questions on the text. You can write short answers – you needn't write complete sentences.

1 Where do the children at AvH come from?

___

2 Where can the children learn German?

___

3 What languages can the students at AvH learn?

___

4 What do the little ones do when they sleep in the school?

___

5 What is special about years 8 and 9?

___

6 What can visitors to the Open House see? (Write three facts.)

___

[1] (to) offer ['ɒfə] *anbieten*   [2] nationality [ˌnæʃə'nælәti] *Nationalität*

LANGUAGE

____ / 36

1 WORDS A school discussion

____ / 9

Last week there was a discussion at AvH School about teenagers and their parents.
Here you find some of the statements.
Complete them with the words from the box.
There are two words in the box that you don't need.

agree • blame for • dialogue • disagree • easy-going • modern • old-fashioned • per • smoke • strict • traditional

1 Twenty years ago family life in Canada was very ____________________.

2 Parents were ____________________ and children had to help a lot in the house.

3 Today family life is very ____________________ in many ways.

4 My parents are ____________________, but sometimes a bit ____________________.

5 Many parents ____________________ with their children about how long they should be allowed to watch TV.

6 You can't ____________________ the children ____________________ modern technology.

7 Children should know ____________________ how long they are allowed to play computer games.

8 One hour ____________________ day in front of the computer is enough.

2 GRAMMAR Information for the school camp

___ / 11

a) *Year 7 is going away for three days, so the teachers give the students some information:*

Dear students and parents,

Here is some information for our school camp:

You can bring your guitars but please don't bring your MP3 players to the camp.

Of course you can play football and volleyball but please don't play before breakfast.

Smoking and drinking alcohol are strictly forbidden[1].

You can spend your free time alone or with your friends.

Don't stay away from the camp for longer than one hour.

There will be a German group at the camp too. So you can make new friends and speak German.

We hope we will have a lot of fun.

Your teachers

*Now write what the students **will be allowed to do** and what they **won't be allowed to do**. What **will they be able to do**? (8P)*

1 The students ______________________ their guitars

but they ______________________ their MP3 players.

2 They ______________________ football and volleyball

but they ______________________ before breakfast.

3 The students ______________________ or ______________________ alcohol.

4 They ______________________ some time alone or with friends.

5 The students ______________________ away from the camp for more than an hour.

6 They ______________________ new friends and talk to them in German.

be able to / be allowed to
Das Ersatzverb **be able to** steht für „können" und das Ersatzverb **be allowed to** steht für „dürfen".
Allowed klingt ein bisschen wie das deutsche Wort Erlaubnis. Und eine Erlaubnis wird gegeben, wenn man etwas darf. Diese Eselsbrücke soll dir Verwechslungen ersparen.

[1] forbidden [fə'bɪdn] *verboten*

b) *Remember when you went on a school trip with your class. What were/weren't you allowed to do? What were you able to do? Write three sentences. Use* ***allowed to / not allowed to*** *and* ***able to / not able to****. (3P)*

The pictures may help you:

1 We were ______________________________

2 ______________________________

3 ______________________________

3 GRAMMAR Open House at AvH

______ /8

Silvy has written an article about the Open House at her school for the school magazine.
Fill in the correct reflexive pronoun or a dash (–) if you don't need one.

The Open House on 16 March was a really exciting day at Alexander von Humboldt School. My class met ______________ at 8 am with our form teacher Mrs Silver. She wanted to show the visitors how we prepare ______________ for tests. Before the lesson started I asked ______________ if this would be interesting for our visitors. But it was! First we felt ______________ a bit strange. But it was OK later. Form 8 HD presented their project "First steps in the kitchen". They have learned how to cook ______________ some easy meals. Another project showed how you can protect ______________ from a bear. Simon from Year 9 showed some of his exciting skateboarding tricks and told the visitors that he had taught ______________ how to skateboard. I think that all the visitors enjoyed ______________ at our Open House. So it was worth getting up so early.

Reflexive pronouns (Reflexivpronomen)

I	myself	(ich) mir/mich	it	itself	(er/sie/es) sich
you	yourself	(du) dir/dich	we	ourselves	(wir) uns
he	himself	(er) sich	you	yourselves	(ihr) euch
she	herself	(sie) sich	they	themselves	(sie) sich

4 GRAMMAR Activities at AvH

____/8

Many classes at AvH have got plans for the rest of the school year.
The notice board tell the school about these plans.

a) *Write sentences about the different plans:*

Year 5 is doing a project about bears next week.

Year 7 ____________________

Year 8 ____________________

Years 3 and 4 ____________________

Year 1 ____________________

Year 6 ____________________

☞
- Wenn du über **feste Pläne** oder **Verabredungen** in der Zukunft sprichst, kannst du das **present progressive** verwenden: *I'm going to Ashley party at the weekend.*
- Um deutlich zu machen, dass es sich um zukünftige Pläne handelt, musst du Zeitangaben verwenden, z. B. *on Friday, next week, at the weekend, tomorrow …*

b) Now you

What are your plans for the next two weeks? Write 3 sentences. The photos may help you. (3P)

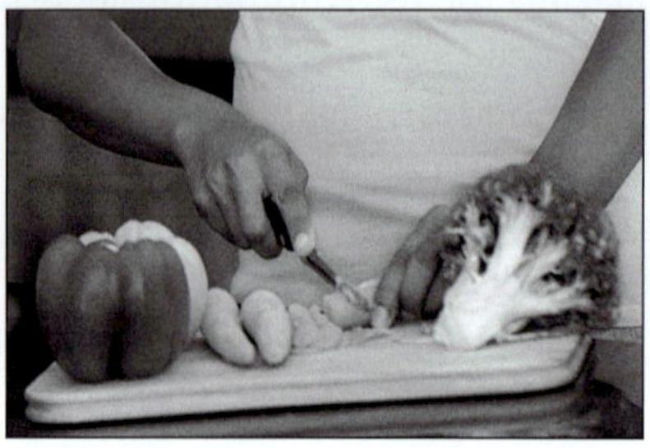

1 ____________________

2 ____________________

3 ____________________

WRITING

____/ 20

An e-mail about a school trip

Your German school has got a partner school in Canada. You often write e-mails to each other about what happens at your school. Today you want to tell the Canadian students about your last school trip.

Write about
– where you went, your journey, where you stayed
– what it was like, the people, what you were allowed / not allowed to do, the food, your teachers

Write about 100 words. Use the simple past.

Steps of Writing

Rufe dir die Schritte beim Verfassen eines Textes in Erinnerung:

1. Vor dem Schreiben: Brainstorming
   - Sammle zunächst alle Ideen, die dir einfallen, z. B. in einer Mindmap oder einer Liste.
   - Wähle dann die besten Ideen aus und ordne sie.
2. Während des Schreibens:
   - Benutze treffende Adjektive: *strict, easy-going, excellent, …*
   - Benutze Relativsätze mit *who* und *that.*
   - Benutze time phrases: *at 7 o'clock, every morning, in the afternoon(s), a few minutes later, suddenly, then, next.*
   - Benutze Konjunktionen: *although, and, because, but, so … that, when, while.*
   - Denke daran, einen Absatz zu machen, wenn du mit einer neuen Idee anfängst.
3. Nach dem Schreiben:
   - Überprüfe, ob dein Text verständlich ist.
   - Überprüfe die Rechtschreibung.
   - Überprüfe die Verbformen (z. B. simple past) und die Wortstellung.

You can start like this:

Dear friends,
Today we want to tell you about our trip to …

Klassenarbeit B

Gesamtpunktzahl ohne Speaking	_____ / 65	Note _____
Gesamtpunktzahl mit Speaking	_____ / 83	Note _____

LISTENING

_____ / 21

10/11 New contest[1] at Radio CBC 1, Montreal

New word
(to) protect [prə'tekt] *schützen*

10 1 Kids' Club on Radio CBC 1

_____ / 5

Listen to Radio CBC 1. You are going to hear a report about a contest for children.

a) *At Victoria School, Toronto, three different classes are working on different projects. Tick (✔) which class is working on the Radio CBC 1 contest.*

One class is writing a diary about their two-week camp near Ontario.	☐
One class is making posters about how people can use public transport[2] more often and in this way help to keep the air of our country clean.	☐
One class is working on a musical about the life of young people in Canada.	☐

b) *Listen again. Tick (✔) the right box.*

1 Radio CBC 1 has a contest	a) every month.	☐
	b) twice a year.	☐
	c) every year.	☐
	d) every 2nd year.	☐

2 The contest is for kids	a) from 6 to 12.	☐
	b) from 6 to 16.	☐
	c) from 10 to 16.	☐
	d) in form 6.	☐

3 You can hand in	a) films.	☐
	b) computer shows.	☐
	c) stories and poems.	☐
	d) interviews.	☐

4 You will get more information about the contest	a) on their website.	☐
	b) in the next show.	☐
	c) from the radio's magazine.	☐
	d) if you write an e-mail.	☐

[1] contest ['kɒntest] *Wettbewerb* [2] public transport [ˌpʌblɪk 'trænspɔːt] *öffentliche Verkehrsmittel*

11 2 At Victoria School, Toronto

____ / 16

Mrs Riley, form teacher of year 7 at Victoria School, Toronto, is talking about the contest to her students.

***a)** What is Mrs Riley talking about to her class? Tick (✔) **Yes** or **No**. (6P)*

Mrs Riley is talking about ...	Yes	No
the rules[1] for writing.		
when they can use the computer room.		
when they can talk to their Art teacher.		
the rules for painting and drawing.		
what students have to do in class and at home.		
the prizes.		

***b)** Listen again. Answer these questions. Write short answers. You don't have to write complete sentences.*

☞ Lies die Fragen vor dem Hören und markiere dir in jeder Frage Schlüsselwörter, die dir helfen, die gewünschte Information aus dem Hörtext herauszufiltern.

1 What is important when you want to write something? (Write two things.) (4P)

____

2 What are you not allowed to do? (3P)

____

3 By when do you need to hand in your work at school? (1P)

____

4 What are the prizes for the national winners? (2P)

____

LANGUAGE

____ / 30

1 WORDS Paraphrased words

____ / 5

Somebody paraphrased these words. Can you find them?

1 It's something you find in a theatre: ______________

2 It's something you get when you want to pay in a restaurant: ______________

3 After you have written a text or a story and you want to make it even better, this is what you do: ______________

4 It's something you might come through when you're canoeing: ______________

5 It's a person who is a boss: ______________

[1] rule [ruːl] *Regel, Vorschrift*

2 WORDS Free time in Canada

___ / 10

a) *Find six words for free-time acitivites in the word square below and mark them. Write down the nouns with the correct verbs:* ***go, have, play****. (6P)*

1 You can go ______________________________.

2 You can ______________________________

3 You can ______________________________

4 You can ______________________________

5 You can ______________________________

6 You can ______________________________

D	E	V	H	Z	K	N	R	S	I	O	M	C	G
D	D	C	A	M	P	I	N	G	G	H	A	A	L
A	S	C	X	V	B	J	Z	T	M	N	L	N	P
Q	N	F	F	E	R	S	T	Z	U	I	M	O	L
Y	O	C	D	H	U	N	T	I	N	G	U	E	P
B	W	N	T	R	D	V	O	H	L	N	N	I	I
A	S	V	F	R	Z	Z	U	O	E	T	C	N	B
W	H	W	Q	R	T	B	C	C	A	O	L	G	K
K	O	H	T	R	E	G	F	K	M	M	L	P	B
B	E	E	W	Q	F	D	S	E	V	C	M	N	Z
Z	I	T	R	F	V	N	O	Y	A	E	R	T	O
F	N	F	S	L	E	E	P	O	V	E	R	S	N
A	G	F	G	H	J	K	B	N	M	Z	U	U	O

b) *Now think of the students at Victoria School in Toronto. Write four sentences and say what the classes did last year. (4P)*

Example:

Last February Year 7 went snowshoeing in the mountains.

1 Last July Year 8 ______________________________

2 ______________________________

3 ______________________________

4 ______________________________

3 GRAMMAR Lunch break at Victoria School

_____ /5

Look at the picture and say what the students are doing or saying. Use ***reflexive pronouns*** *and* ***each other****.*

1 The girl is talking to ______________________.

2 Two girls are teaching ______________________ Maths.

3 Two girls are hiding ______________________ from the camera of a boy.

4 One boy is making ______________________ a sandwich.

5 "I can see ______________________ in the mirror," the girl at the table says.

4 GRAMMAR Anna and her Canadian friend Janet

_____ /5

Anna from Hanover has a Canadian online friend in Toronto. Her name is Janet.
Complete the sentences with ***each other*** *and* ***themselves****.*

1 Almost every week they write e-mails to ______________________.

2 They both want to learn Spanish, but they can't take Spanish at school. So they have got a Spanish book and a CD. They are teaching ______________________ Spanish.

3 Sometimes they even chat with ______________________ in Spanish.

4 Today Anna wants a photo of Janet and Janet wants a photo of Anna. So they take photos of ______________________ and send them to ______________________ via e-mail.

☞ sich = sich gegenseitig, einander ▸ **each other**
sich = sich selbst ▸ **themselves**

5 GRAMMAR Working for the contest

____/5

Pete, Joel and Amy write a report for the contest 'Saving energy' on Radio CBC 1. They write about public transport[1] in Canada. Here is their calendar with all the tasks they ***have to do*** *this week.*

Monday 11th April	Tuesday 12th April	Wednesday 13th April	Thursday 14th April today	Friday 15th April
Pete and Joel: interview people in the city of Toronto	**Amy:** draw pictures of buses in Toronto	**Amy and Joel:** talk to students about school buses	**Pete and Joel:** write the report **Amy:** find pictures for the report	**Pete, Joel and Amy:** no work on the report!

Verwende zwei verschiedene Zeiten:
simple past für Dinge, die die Schüler bereits erledigt haben,
will-future für Dinge, die die Schüler noch erledigen müssen.

1 On Monday Pete and Joel had to interview people in the city of Toronto.

2 On Tuesday Amy ______________________________.

3 ______________________________

4 ______________________________. (2P)

5 ______________________________

[1] public transport [ˌpʌblɪk ˈtrænspɔːt] *öffentliche Verkehrsmittel*

MEDIATION

___/14

A contest in Germany

Sport an eurer Schule

Das Thema unseres diesjährigen Wettbewerbs ist „Sport an eurer Schule".
Teilnehmen können alle Schülerinnen und Schüler im Alter von 10 bis 16 Jahren.

Ihr könnt

★ über den Sportunterricht an eurer Schule berichten (wann findet er statt, wie oft, was macht ihr im Sportunterricht, was habt ihr für Verbesserungsvorschläge?).
★ eine Geschichte über ein lustiges Ereignis während des Sportunterrichts schreiben.
★ einen Bericht über ein wichtiges sportliches Ereignis an eurer Schule schreiben.
★ ein Interview mit einem Schüler / einer Schülerin machen, der/die eine Lieblingssportart hat. Erstellt eine Tondatei des Interviews oder schreibt es auf.
★ ein Poster zum Thema Schulsport anfertigen.

Ihr dürft in Teams zu zweit arbeiten. Eure Arbeit muss mit Computer geschrieben sein.
Das Poster soll farbig sein. Sprecht mit euren Sport- und Kunstlehrern über diesen Wettbewerb. Sie helfen euch sicherlich gerne weiter.
Eure Beiträge müssen bis 1. Juni bei unserem Fußballverein sein.

Preise:
★ Nehmen alle Schüler/Schülerinnen einer Klasse teil, so bekommt jeder ein kleines Geschenk.
★ Gewinne

1.–3. Preis	je eine Jahreskarte für alle Fußballspiele unseres Vereins
4.–10. Preis	je zwei Eintrittskarten für ein Fußballspiel deiner Wahl
11.–20. Preis	je eine Eintrittskarte für ein Fußballspiel deiner Wahl

Wir freuen uns auf eure Beiträge und auf euch!!!
Eure Jugendabteilung des Fußballvereins FC 2020

Phil is an exchange student from Canada in your form. Your form is working on a contest and you're explaining the topic and the rules[1] to your friend from Canada.

Wenn dir ein Wort auf Englisch nicht einfällt, versuche es zu umschreiben:
It's somebody who ... It's something that ... It's a place where ...

Phil I'm interested in your contest. Is it right that everybody must write a report about PE at your school?

You Well, you can write a report but you can do other things too.

Phil So, what are the other things? (4 things)

You ______________________________ (2P)

Phil That sounds interesting. Who can you interview then?

You ______________________________ (2P)

Phil And how are you going to send them the interview? (2 things)

You ______________________________ (2P)

Phil What is the first prize?

You ______________________________ (2P)

Phil Oh, I'd like to win a ticket like that. Who can work on the contest?

You ______________________________ (1P)

Phil I'd like to make a poster. What are the rules for the poster? (2 things)

You ______________________________ (2P)

Phil What about you? Could we work together?

You ______________________________ (1P)

Phil So, what are we waiting for? Let's go.

WRITING

Da dies eine zusätzliche Writing-Aufgabe ist, wird sie in der Gesamtpunktzahl für Klassenarbeit B nicht gewertet.

____/20

Now you want to write a report for the German contest together with Phil.
You have chosen the topic "A report about a sport event at your school".
Phil wants to send the report to his school magazine in Canada too so you're writing in English.

Write about 80–100 words.

- Bei dieser Aufgabe hast du fast keine Vorgaben, so dass es sehr wichtig ist, dass du die drei Schritte beim Verfassen eines Textes beachtest. Siehe dazu den Hinweis zur Writing-Aufgabe auf S. 49 im Klassenarbeitstrainer.
- Schreibe deine Ideen unbedingt gleich auf Englisch auf, damit du später die notwendigen Wörter schon parat hast.
- Schreibe zunächst einen Entwurf und überprüfe ihn anhand der Checkliste im Lösungsheft auf S. 31.
- Überarbeite dann deinen Entwurf solange, bis du ganz zufrieden bist.

[1] rule [ru:l] *Regel, Vorschrift*

SPEAKING

____/18

12 An interview for the contest[1]

Phil likes the idea of the contest so much that he is doing some interviews too. Listen to his interview with Kira.

New word
(to) come fifth *fünfter werden (bei einem Wettbewerb)*

13 Now you

Now Phil is interviewing Alexander, who is good at skiing. Imagine you are Alexander and are answering Phil's questions. Please make notes before you start with the interview. You can use the notepad below.

Höre dir zunächst Phils Fragen an und überlege mit Hilfe des Notizzettels, was du antworten kannst. Um hilfreiche Formulierungen zu finden, kannst du dir noch einmal das Interview mit Kira anhören.
Höre dir dann die Fragen ein zweites Mal an und beantworte sie. Drücke die Pausentaste, damit du genügend Zeit für deine Antworten hast.

Your notes:

1 **About myself**

– how old ____________________

– where from ____________________

– favourite sport *skiing*

– started with this sport when ____________________

2 **contests**

– local[2] contests: where/when ____________________

– all-German contests: where/when ____________________

3 **training**

–howoften ____________________

–howlong ____________________

[1] contest ['kɒntest] *Wettbewerb* [2] local ['ləʊkl] *Orts-, örtlich*

Klassenarbeit A

Gesamtpunktzahl ______ / 54 Note ______

READING

______ / 13

An article for TEEN MAGAZINE

1 STUDY SKILLS Skimming

______ / 1

Nathalie L'Estane, one of the editors of TEEN MAGAZINE, has just got a new article for the fashion section. She skims the text to find out what it is about. Then she writes down one sentence about the article in her notes. Complete her sentence.

The article "My dream job: fashion designer" is about ______________________________

____

____

My dream job: fashion designer

Many things can help to get into a fashion school

by Simon Pey

Fashion designer – sounds like a dream job, eh? Well, it's my dream job, so I tried to get as much information as I could. I read many articles in books and magazines.
Last month I was able to talk to a British fashion designer who is a friend of my father's. So I got first-class information, if you know what I mean. And I thought it might be helpful for some of you too, so I want to share my information with you. Here is what I have found out so far:

There are quite a number of fashion schools in Great Britain. But the first thing you must know about them is that it's really difficult to get into one of them. You have to work really hard before a good fashion school will accept[1] you as a student. But here is the good news: if you really want to be a fashion designer and go to a fashion school there are things you can do. Here are some ideas for you:

1 Take a class in drawing at your school. It's best if you draw real people – if this is not possible, start drawing from photos of fashion models. Also learn about colours. You should know what colours look good together. Then draw your fashion ideas and keep your drawings in your portfolio[2] – you might need them later!

[1] accept [ək'sept] *hier: aufnehmen* [2] portfolio [pɔːt'fəʊliəʊ] *Mappe für Zeichnungen*

2 Learn to make clothes. First make clothes for yourself and then for your friends. Maybe your friends will even give you some money for the clothes – if they look good.

3 Find out about trendy fashion. Visit websites about fashion to see what colours are going to be the fashion. Think about what will be popular next year.

4 Learn about fashion in earlier centuries. Get to know old fashion styles likes those from the Victorian Age[1]. Have a look at clothes from the 1950s, 1960s, ... until today. Also find out about the important 20th-century designers like Chanel and Dior.

5 Learn how companies sell their fashion. What are the big department stores in your city? What shops sell the kind of fashion you are interested in? Find out about the customers that buy these clothes. Who are they, how old are they, what job have they got, what do they do in their free time?

If you have more information or questions, just write an e-mail to: simon@pey.cim
I hope to hear from you soon.

2 Susan needs information

____ / 6

Susan (14) from Toronto wants to be a fashion designer. She has many questions.
When Susan reads the article "My dream job: fashion designer", she gets answers to ***six*** *of her questions.*
Tick (✔) these ***six*** *questions.*

1 Where are the really good fashion schools?	
2 What things can I do that will help me to get into a fashion school?	
3 Can I do something at my school?	
4 Do I need a lot of money to be a fashion designer?	
5 Will I need my own computer?	
6 How can I find out about the latest fashion?	
7 What can I put into my portfolio?	
8 Will I have to learn to make clothes?	
9 Will I easily find a job?	
10 Will I have to search the internet for information?	

[1] Victorian Age [vɪk'tɔ:riən ˌeɪdʒ] *im Zeitalter von Königin Victoria (1837–1901)*

3 About Simon's article

___ / 6

Choose the answer that fits best.

1 Simon got his information from	a) magazines and his father.	
	b) books and the internet.	
	c) magazines and a fashion designer.	

2 It's not easy	a) to find a place in a fashion school.	
	b) to find out about the latest fashion.	
	c) to find information about a job as a fashion designer.	

3 In your portfolio you can put	a) the clothes you have made.	
	b) the latest fashion magazines.	
	c) your best fashion drawings.	

4 If you make clothes,	a) they must fit.	
	b) you should only make them for other people.	
	c) you might get some money.	

5 Find out about	a) fashion of different countries.	
	b) fashion of the past and today.	
	c) famous fashion labels.	

6 If you go to department stores,	a) study the customers there.	
	b) look around for good clothes.	
	c) find out about the companies that sell their clothes there.	

LANGUAGE

____ / 25

1 WORDS An alphabetical list

____ / 17

a) *The letters of the new words are mixed up. Put them in the correct order and write the words into the list. (9P)*

A	ecnuanon	N	
B	**isabgppe**	O	eotpear
C	earrce	P	eipp
D	gwaidnr	Q	
E	dretoi	R	erdidl
F		S	escuscs
G	og ornwg	T	uent
H	dohhaeensp	U	suulfe
I		V	**noaatcvi**
J		W	ewka pu
K	peke	X	
L	reehlat	Y	
M	**aiucsnim**	Z	

b) *Think of* ***five*** *more new words that you have learned in Unit 5. (5P)*

1 ____

2 ____

3 ____

4 ____

5 ____

c) *Paraphrase the words in bold print from* ***1a****. (3P)*

☞ Erkläre die Wörter mit einfachen englischen Sätzen.

1 ____

2 ____

3 ____

2 GRAMMAR At a London fashion school

_____ /8

Some students at a London fashion school are talking about their plans for this summer.

Write down what they are doing this summer. (5P)

1 In July, Jimmy is ______________________________.

2 In June, Sue ______________________________.

3 ______________________________

4 ______________________________

5 ______________________________

Now you

Write about your plans for the summer. (3P)

1 ______________________________

2 ______________________________

3 ______________________________

☞
- Wenn du über **feste Pläne** oder **Verabredungen** in der Zukunft sprichst, kannst du das **present progressive** verwenden: *I'**m going** to Ashley's party at the weekend.*
- Um deutlich zu machen, dass es sich um zukünftige Pläne handelt, musst du Zeitangaben verwenden, z. B. *in July, on Friday, next week, at the weekend, tomorrow …*
- Bildung *present progressive*:
  am/is/are + ing-form: *I'**m going** on a cycle tour next weekend.*

[1] company ['kʌmpəni] *Firma*

MEDIATION

____ / 16

☞ Beachte, dass du bei der Sprachmittlung einen Rollenwechsel vornehmen musst:
Deine Mutter sagt z.B.: *„Frag sie, wie lange* ***sie*** *schon in Deutschland sind."*
Sprichst du dann zu der anderen Person, wird aus dem **sie** im Deutschen ein **you** im Englischen: *How long have* ***you*** *been in Germany?*
Das Gleiche gilt für dein Dolmetschen vom Englischen ins Deutsche.

A Canadian family in Germany

You are on a day trip with your parents near your hometown. You get to know a Canadian family. Because your parents don't speak very much English you help with the conversation.

Your mum Frag sie, wie lange sie schon in Deutschland sind und wie lange sie noch bleiben.

You ______________________________ (2P)

Woman We have been here for two weeks and we are staying until the end of the month.

You ______________________________ (2P)

Your mum Frag sie, wo sie hier wohnen.

You ______________________________ (1P)

Woman We are staying in a holiday apartment. It's small but we like it very much.
It's good because we can cook our own meals. So we needn't go to a restaurant every day.

You ______________________________

____

______________________________ (3P)

Your mum Frag sie mal, ob sie noch Ideen für Ausflüge brauchen.

You ______________________________ (2P)

Woman Well, we have seen quite a lot of this area really. We want to visit one or two museums.
Can you give us an idea where we could go?

You ______________________________

____

______________________________ (3P)

→

Your mum Wie wäre es, wenn wir die Familie in den nächsten Tagen zum Kaffee zu uns nach Hause einladen? Dann können wir ihre Pläne besprechen und werden etwas Gutes finden. Und ich backe einen guten deutschen Kuchen.

You ____

____

____ (3P)

Woman Thank you so much. We would like to come and of course we all like German cake.

Gesamtpunktzahl ohne Speaking ______ / 56 Note ______	
Gesamtpunktzahl mit Speaking ______ / 71 Note ______	

LISTENING

______ / 15

14 At Brandon's office

Brandon, the main editor of TEEN MAGAZINE, is sitting in his office. A lot of people call him today. Listen to the telephone calls.

1 HEADLINES[1] in the next TEEN MAGAZINE

______ / 7

Listen to the telephone calls. In the next TEEN MAGAZINE you will find ***seven*** *of these headlines. Tick (✔) them.*

5 minutes that will keep you fit	☐	Susan – queen of girls' football	☐
Latest films at Toronto cinemas	☐	When did YOU last go to the cinema?	☐
My visit to a cinema in New York	☐	A report about Maths at school	☐
A first-class concert 50 students sing	☐	A report about my favourite singer	☐
An interview with a pilot	☐	Power learning	☐
Great fashion show at high school	☐	THIS YEAR AT THE BEACH	☐
101 socks	☐		

[1] headline ['hedlaɪn] *Schlagzeile*

2 About the calls

_____ /8

a) *Listen again to each of the telephone calls. Tick (✔) the correct box. (4P)*

First call

1 Mitsu is not sure about Paul's article	a) because she doesn't know Paul.	
	b) because Paul has written about a very old film.	
	c) because you can't see the film in Canada.	
	d) because she already has many articles.	

Second call

2 Jeff	a) wants to talk about a concert.	
	b) wants to talk to Robert.	
	c) is a friend of Brandon.	
	d) wants to call again on Friday.	

Third call

3 Lisa	a) calls because she wants to open a new section for TEEN MAGAZINE.	
	b) says she is a successful learner.	
	c) asks if she can come to Brandon's office.	
	d) hasn't got time this week.	

Fourth call

4 Nathalie	a) talks about the best beaches.	
	b) is quite happy about the articles in her section.	
	c) doesn't have enough articles.	
	d) has already sent her material to Brandon.	

b) *Listen again to all four telephone calls. Tick (✔) the **four** correct sentences. (4P)*

Brandon	1) thinks the new magazine will be good.	
	2) thinks Paul's article is boring.	
	3) knows the Chinese film Paul has seen.	
	4) doesn't know Robert's telephone number.	
	5) likes Lisa's idea.	
	6) will meet Lisa tomorrow.	
	7) rings up Nathalie.	
	8) wants Nathalie's material by tomorrow.	

LANGUAGE

____/16

1 WORDS An article in TEEN MAGAZINE

____/12

This is an article for the music section in the latest TEEN MAGAZINE. Fill in the missing words. There are four more words in the box than you need. Use the underlined verbs in the correct tense (simple past or will-future).

caption • career • company • be sold out • biography • bold print • opera • musician • office • record • release • silence • success • successful • useful • vacation

Becoming a star

Hi, my name is Michael Howell and I'm 15 years old. I'm quite a good singer and I can play the guitar well. When you play a musical instrument, you always dream of a big ____________ as a ____________. Sometimes I already see my name in ____________ in the newspaper together with a photo and a ____________: "Michael Howell – a story of ____________". So when I heard about an audition[1] for a new CD with songs from local teenagers I went there. I had to go to the ____________ of the ____________ first and tell them some facts about myself. That was for a short ____________. Then the big moment came: I went into the studio and played and sang two songs. They ____________ them. They will tell me in a few days if one of my songs will be on the CD. I hope that I was ____________. They ____________ the CD in summer. So keep your eyes open – I think it ____________ soon.

2 Getting by in English

____/4

Write what you would say in English.

Was sagst du, ...

1 ... wenn du möchtest, dass jemand seine Augen offen halten soll?

____

2 ... wenn du sagen willst: „Das liegt bei dir."?

____

3 ... deiner Freundin / deinem Freund, wenn du denkst, dass jemand in sie/ihn verknallt ist?

____

4 ... wenn du gut in Mathe bist?

____

[1] audition [ɔːˈdɪʃn] *Casting/Vorspiel*

WRITING

___/25

1 Correcting mistakes

___/5

Read the following text carefully and find the five mistakes. Then rewrite the text.

Überprüfe den Text auf folgende Fehlerkategorien hin:
- Rechtschreibfehler – **S** (Groß-, Kleinschreibung, fehlende Buchstaben bei einem Wort, richtige Schreibweise bei der Pluralbildung: shelf – shelves; family – families)
- Wortstellung – **WO** (im Englischen: subject – verb – object)
- Ist es das richtige Wort? – **W** (z. B.: Handy ≠ handy, sondern: mobile phone)

About my favourite star – a quiz

My favourite star is a man. He was born in england in 1982 (**S**). When he was five years old, he became his first guitar from his father (**W**). He started to play and soon he was quite good. He learned to sing too.

His friends liked his music. Very often they asked him to play at partys (**S**). When he was 18 he played his first concert and at the age of 22 released he his first CD (**WO**). It was a sucess (**S**).

Can you guess who it is?

2 New editors for TEEN MAGAZINE

_____ / 20

In Unit 4 hast du dich intensiv mit kreativen Schreibaufgaben befasst. Auf S. 49 im Aufgabenteil und auf S. 31 im Lösungsteil findest du Checklisten für vor und nach dem Schreiben eines Textes. Sieh dort noch einmal nach, worauf du achten musst, bevor du diese Aufgabe beginnst.

Dear readers of TEEN MAGAZINE,

We want to start new sections for TEEN MAGAZINE and are looking for motivated young editors. You'll find some ideas for a new section here:

problem letters • quiz page • new games • computer world • about Canada • holidays

Are you interested or have you got any other ideas? If so, please send an e-mail to us: brandon@teenmagazine.cim

You want to start a new section for TEEN MAGAZINE.
Write an e-mail to Brandon with the following information:

- write about who you are
- write about the section you would like to start (you may choose from the box or add a new idea)
- give details about your ideas for this section (possible articles, ...)
- give your full name, address and phone number

Write about 100 words.

SPEAKING

____/15

Brandon's answering machine[1]

15

Brandon is the main editor of TEEN MAGAZINE. He can't be in his office this afternoon. So a lot of people leave a message for him on the answering machine. Listen to the messages.

Höre dir die Nachrichten ein zweites Mal an und notiere dir Formulierungen, die hilfreich sind, wenn du in **Now you** selbst eine Nachricht auf einem Anrufbeantworter hinterlässt.

Now you

Three more people leave their messages on the answering machine. Take their role. Give yourself a new name and a new telephone number for each part.

Das englische Alphabet zum Buchstabieren der Namen findest du in deinem Englischbuch auf S. 229.

First caller:
- gives her/his name and spells it
- has got an appointment on ... , but not possible
- says why
- asks for a call back for a new appointment
- gives her/his number

Second caller:
- gives her/his name and spells it
- has written an article about ...
- publish article?
- asks for a call back – gives her/his number

Third caller:
- gives her/his name
- has got more information about two young Germans who were in Montreal last month
- gives the name of one of them, spells the name and gives the telephone number
- says he is waiting for call

[1] answering machine ['ɑːnsərɪŋ məʃiːn] *Anrufbeantworter*

EXAM SKILLS

How to do well in a test

Countdown zum Testerfolg

Ein Test ist angekündigt? Kein Grund zur Panik. Wichtig ist, dass du weißt, worauf du dich vorbereiten musst. Im Zweifelsfall frag deine Lehrerin oder deinen Lehrer. Der Countdown kann beginnen!

Eine Woche vor dem Test

1 Lies noch einmal die **Texte** der zuletzt durchgenommenen Unit (A-Section und Text, eventuell auch das Background File). Fasse mündlich oder schriftlich zusammen, worum es ging.

2 Wiederhole den **Wortschatz** der Unit mit Hilfe des *Vocabulary* oder des *Wordmaster*.
Schreibe dir die Wörter und Wortverbindungen, die du immer wieder vergisst, auf ein Blatt Papier.
Eine Mindmap oder ein Wortfeld helfen beim Behalten.

3 Geh auch noch mal die neue **Grammatik** durch. Aufgaben zur Selbstüberprüfung und zum Üben findest du im *Practice*-Teil, auf der Seite „How am I doing?“, im *Grammar File* (S. 172-189), in deinem *Workbook* und im *e-Workbook*.

Zwei Tage vor dem Test

1 Wiederhole den **Wortschatz**. Manche Wörter sitzen noch nicht? Schreibe einen kurzen Text, in dem du sie verwendest.

2 Lies die **Texte** ein weiteres Mal.

3 Erkläre einem Freund oder einer Freundin die neue **Grammatik**. Das klappt nicht richtig? Dann lies nochmal im *Grammar File* nach.

Am Abend vor dem Test

1 Entspanne dich. Du kannst lesen, dich in die Badewanne legen, Musik hören, fernsehen, ...

2 Geh zur gewohnten Zeit ins Bett.

Am Morgen des Tests

1 Steh rechtzeitig auf, damit du nicht hetzen musst.

2 Lies irgendetwas „zum Aufwärmen“, aber schau nicht mehr in dein Schülerbuch.

Während des Tests

1 Denk daran: Du hast dich gut vorbereitet. Es gibt keinen Grund, nervös zu sein.

2 Konzentriere dich auf den Test, lass dich nicht ablenken.

3 Lies dir die Aufgaben genau durch. Dann löse zuerst die Aufgaben, die dir einfach scheinen. Wende dich erst danach den schwereren Aufgaben zu.

4 Aufgaben, die du bearbeitet hast, hakst du ab. So siehst du, wie du vorankommst, und behältst den Überblick.

5 Schau ab und zu auf die Uhr. Du solltest dir für den Schluss noch etwas Zeit einplanen, um deine Antworten noch einmal durchzulesen und wenn nötig zu korrigieren.

Aufgabenstellungen verstehen

Bevor du anfängst, die Aufgaben zu bearbeiten, vergewissere dich, dass du genau weißt, was du tun sollst. Lies die Aufgabe Wort für Wort langsam und gründlich und von Anfang bis Ende durch. Du kannst besonders wichtige Teile der Aufgabenstellung unterstreichen und die Aufgabe, wenn nötig, für dich in einzelne Schritte unterteilen.

Den folgenden Arbeitsanweisungen begegnest du häufig:

Add Verbinde eine Information oder einen Sachverhalt mit einer/einem anderen auf die geforderte Art und Weise.

Choose Wähle zwischen verschiedenen Möglichkeiten die passende Information aus.

Comment Kommentiere einen Sachverhalt durch die Darstellung deiner eigenen Meinung dazu. Begründe und erläutere sie möglichst genau.

Compare Vergleiche Dinge, Wörter oder Sachverhalte, indem du prüfst, ob und auf welche Weise sie gleiche oder verschiedene Eigenschaften, Aussehen, Bedeutungen oder Funktionen haben.

Complete Ergänze eine Information, indem du sie an dem dafür vorgesehenen Platz einträgst und damit z. B. einen Satz sinnvoll beendest.

Describe Beschreibe ein Objekt oder eine Person, d.h. stelle dar, wie sie aussehen, wie das Objekt funktioniert oder die Personen handeln. Vermeide eigene Wertungen wie z. B. „beautiful", „useful" oder „great".

Discuss Diskutiere ein Thema, eine Behauptung oder eine Aussage. Untersuche möglichst viele Seiten davon, z. B. Vor- und Nachteile, und stelle diese geordnet dar.

Explain Erkläre einen Sachverhalt, d. h. gib wesentliche Fakten über ihn und erläutere, wie sie logisch zusammenhängen.

Fill in Trage die geforderten Informationen in den dafür vorgesehenen Platz ein, z. B. in eine Lücke oder eine Tabelle.

List Schreibe einzelne oder mehrere Informationen übersichtlich und geordnet auf, z. B. in einer Reihe, Tabelle oder einem anderen Verzeichnis.

Listen Höre dir einen Text, einzelne Informationen oder Sachverhalte an.

Match Ordne die angegebenen Informationen einander zu, wie es die Aufgabe erfordert. Finde z. B. Satzanfänge und passende Satzenden und füge sie zusammen.

Use Verwende eine Tatsache, ein Wort usw. so, wie es in der Aufgabe gefordert wird.

Write a ... Schreibe etwas in einem geforderten Textformat auf, z. B. deinen Kommentar zu etwas oder eine Geschichte.

Erweiterte Ausgabe D3

English G 21

Klassenarbeitstrainer

für Schülerinnen und Schüler

Lösungen und Lerntipps

Cornelsen

Lösungen A

LISTENING

Going to London

01 Text 1

Reporter Hi everybody, you're listening to Radio Rainbow. Here we are again on this sunny afternoon. I hope you're all well and excited to hear more about last week's quiz, the answer and – of course – to find out who is today's winner. Did you send an answer too? Then maybe you are going to win a weekend in London. You never know – maybe you are today's winner.
Well – last week our show was about planning a trip to London, so of course our question was about London. We wanted to know: When did Queen Victoria open Victoria Park in London and what did people call it at that time? We got over 500 answers, and 438 of them were right. Congratulations.
While we listen to some more music I'll try to phone the lucky winner. So if your phone rings in a minute, you'll be on your way to London soon ...

Reporter Hello, this is Tom from Radio Rainbow. Am I talking to Chris Benson?

Chris Hello Tom. Yes, I'm Chris. Have I really ...?

Reporter Well Chris, you sent an e-mail with the two correct answers. Chris, please tell our listeners: When did Queen Victoria open Victoria Park?

Chris Er ... She opened the park in 1845.

Reporter Yes, you're right. 1845 is the correct answer. And what did people call it at that time?

Chris They often called it the "People's Park". But don't ask me why they called it that, I can't remember.

Reporter But you had the right answers in your e-mail and so you are today's winner. Congratulations!! Now Chris, let's talk about you. I think you are quite young. How old are you?

Chris Yeah, you're right, I'm only 14 and I'm still at school.

Reporter Well, you're still young but you are old enough to go to London, I think. Let's listen to some more music before we talk about your trip.

02 Text 2

Reporter Chris, you've won a long weekend from Friday to Sunday in a four-star hotel in London for two people. Who will you take with you? Do you already know?

Chris Well, I haven't thought about it really, but I could take my mum or my dad.

Reporter Let me explain the details to you. After you arrive at your London hotel on Friday evening, there will be a welcoming dinner in the hotel's restaurant. You will also get your free London travelcards for Saturday and Sunday. You can plan your activities for the weekend just as you like.

Chris Great, I've never been to London before so there will be a lot to visit, I'm sure.

Reporter When you're planning your sightseeing tour for the two days, make sure to leave some time for a boat trip on the River Thames and a visit to the London Eye. You will get your free tickets at the hotel too. Of course Radio Rainbow is paying for your two return tickets for the train. So what about that, Chris?

Chris Oh, I love going by train. I'm really happy and I'm looking forward to going to London. Thank you so much, Tom.

Reporter Well everybody, next week we're going to talk about Wales. So tune in next week – there is a chance for a new winner. Have a good week everybody and bye-bye.

About the radio show

a)

	Right	Wrong
1 There was a quiz on the radio show.	✔	
2 Last week's radio show was about planning a trip to London.	✔	
3 You had to write a report about London to win a prize.		✔
4 Every listener had the right answer.		✔
5 The prize was a ticket for a music festival.		✔
6 You can win something in next week's show.	✔	

b)

Text 1

1 1845, 2 in an e-mail, 3 is a student

Text 2

The reporter talks to Tom about ...

	Yes	No
1 ... the dinner on the first evening.	✔	
2 ... planning the sightseeing tour.	✔	
3 ... shopping in London.		✔
4 ... a boat trip on the River Thames.	✔	
5 ... free tickets for the theatre.		✔
6 ... how Chris will travel to London.	✔	

Lerntipp So kannst du **Listening Skills** üben:

- Markiere dir in der Aufgabenstellung **Schlüsselwörter (key words)**, auf die du im Hörtext achten kannst, um die gesuchte Information zu finden. *(There was a quiz on the radio show.)*
- Höre dir die beiden Listening-Teile noch einmal an.
- Drücke mehrfach die Pausentaste und notiere in Stichpunkten, was dir wichtig für die Beantwortung der Aufgaben erscheint.
- Vergleiche deine Stichpunkte später mit dem abgedruckten Listening-Text auf S. 2 im Lösungsheft.
- Unterstreiche im Listening-Text, was du nicht so gut verstanden hast. Versuche herauszufinden, woran es lag:
  - Waren dir die Wörter unbekannt? ▸ Schlage die Wörter im Dictionary deines Englischbuches auf den S. 181–204 nach und präge sie dir ein.
  - Hast du dir bekannte Wörter nicht wiedererkannt? ▸ Höre dir die Wörter auf der CD noch einmal an und präge dir die Aussprache ein, indem du die Wörter laut nachsprichst.

LANGUAGE

1 WORDS A quiz about transport

1 If you want to fly to Australia, you must go to the airport.

2 Your plane leaves from gate number B34.

3 If you need a ticket for the bus, you can get it from the ticket machine.

4 Another word for the underground in London is the Tube.

5 Let's see which platform the train leaves from.

6 If you go by train and you only go one way, you need a single ticket.

7 The colours on the Tube map show you the different lines.

8 If you put the letters in the correct order, you get a word that has to do with traffic: rush hour.

2 WORDS Word groups

Instruments	Buildings and places in town	Food
fiddle	cathedral	turkey
recorder	square	pork
trumpet	circus/column	beef
flute	lane	onion

3 GRAMMAR Before the weekend in London

1 Chris and his father have already packed their suitcases.

2 Chris's father has already checked the train times.

3 Chris hasn't read the book about London yet.

4 Chris's father has already phoned the hotel in London.

5 They haven't made sandwiches for the train journey yet.

4 GRAMMAR After the trip to London

Mögliche Sätze:

We had breakfast at 8 o'clock on Saturday and Sunday.

We visited the London Eye at 10 o'clock on Saturday.

We went on a boat trip on the River Thames at 12 o'clock on Saturday.

We looked at the dinosaurs in the Natural History Museum at 2 o'clock on Saturday.

We had dinner at a Chinese restaurant at 6 o'clock on Saturday.

We bought two T-shirts at Brick Lane Market at 10 o'clock on Sunday.

We visited Madame Tussauds at 12 o'clock on Sunday.

We relaxed in Hyde Park at 4 o'clock on Sunday.

WRITING

A diary about our trip to London

Lösungsvorschlag

Dear diary,

Mum, Dad, Ron and I started our journey to London this morning. We were very excited (1P) but the journey was long and boring. (1P) I didn't like it because we spent too much time in the car! (2P) When we arrived in London, we didn't find / couldn't find our hotel at first. (2P) Mum was angry with Dad because he didn't have a map of London! (2P) After two hours we found our hotel (1P) – it's super and the rooms are really nice (1P) so everybody was/is happy again. (1P) In the afternoon we visited Buckingham Palace (1P) and then we went to Hyde Park. (1P) Buckingham Palace was quite boring (1P) but I liked Hyde Park (1P) because we all relaxed for an hour. (1P) In the evening we went to an Indian restaurant. (1P) The food was great (1P) – not too spicy and not too mild. (1P)

Now I am very tired. Good night! (1P)

Lerntipp So kannst du **Writing Skills** üben:

- Unterstreiche im Lösungstext die **Konjunktionen** *(but, because)*.
- Unterstreiche oder ergänze diese Wörter in deinem Text. Dazu musst du deinen Text manchmal leicht verändern, indem du die Sätze verbindest.
- Unterstreiche die **Adjektive** *(excited, long, boring, angry, super, nice, happy, great, spicy, mild)* und die **Adverbien** *(very, really)* im Lösungstext und in deiner eigenen Lösung. Vergleiche und ergänze.
- Unterstreiche die **Zeitangaben**: *this morning, when, at first, after two hours, again, in the afternoon, then for an hour, in the evening* im Lösungstext und in deiner eigenen Lösung. Vergleiche und ergänze. Achte darauf, dass du die richtige Satzstellung eingehalten hast: S-V-O: This morning I played football. Nicht: ~~This morning played I football.~~

Lösungen B

READING

Victoria Park

1 About Victoria Park

Bild 1, Bild 2 und Bild 4 sind richtig.

2 Victoria Park now and then

		Right	Wrong	Not in the text
1	Somebody from the Royal Family opened the park.	✔		
2	In 1845 more than 30,000 people wanted a park in the north-east of London.	✔		
3	Victoria Park is the oldest park in London.		✔	
4	Another name for Victoria Park was "People's Park" because many people visited the park every day.		✔	
5	You can still swim in the lakes in Victoria Park today.			✔
6	Today there is a western part and a larger eastern part.	✔		
7	You can watch animals in Victoria Park.	✔		
8	Victoria Park is only interesting for children.		✔	
9	You can only visit Victoria Park during the day.			✔
10	You are not allowed to ride your bike in the park.			✔
11	You are not allowed to drink alcohol at the *Underage Festival*.	✔		
12	You can listen to some of the music from the *Underage Festival* on the radio.	✔		

Lerntipp So kannst du **Reading Skills / Scanning** üben:

- Verschaffe dir zunächst einen **Überblick**, um was es in einem Text geht. Schaue dir dazu Bilder und Überschriften an und lies den Text einmal in Ruhe durch.
- Markiere jetzt in den Aussagen 1–12 **Schlüsselwörter (key words)**, nach denen du im Text über den Victoria Park suchen kannst, um die gesuchte Information zu finden.
  Z.B. für Aussage 1: *Royal Familiy / open*
- Suche dann den Text nach diesen Schlüsselwörtern und den gesuchten Informationen ab. Manchmal ist die Information auch anders verpackt. D. h. die Schlüsselwörter aus der Aufgabenstellung tauchen im Text nicht genau so auf. Sie sind dann umschrieben, weisen aber auch auf die gewünschte Information hin. Hier im Text findest du beispielsweise *Queen* und in der Aufgabenstellung *Royal Family*.

LANGUAGE

1 GRAMMAR Wednesday afternoon at Victoria Park

a)

1 Three boys have played football.

2 The people haven't listened to a concert yet.

3 An old lady has read a book.

4 A mother and her two children have looked at the deer.

5 The man hasn't cut the grass.

6 Two tourists have visited the park.

b)

Mögliche Fragen

Have you read the newspaper yet?

Have you looked at the trees yet?

Have you just talked to other tourists?

Have you had a picnic yet?

Have you played cricket yet?

Have you seen the deer yet?

Have you ever been in London before?

Have you just taken a photo?

Why have you come to Victoria Park?

What have you just done?

Have you just listened to a concert?

2 GRAMMAR About two tourists

1 Ricky and Sue have already visited the London Eye. They visited it on Monday morning.

2 They have already taken the Tube. They took the Tube on Monday afternoon.

3 Ricky has already been to Big Ben. He was there on Tuesday afternoon.

4 Sue has been shopping at a market. She went shopping on Tuesday afternoon.

5 They have had dinner at an Indian restaurant. They had dinner there on Tuesday evening.

6 They have been on a boat trip on the River Thames. They were there on Wednesday afternoon.

Lerntipp So findest du heraus: **present perfect** oder **simple past**?

Markiere alle Signalwörter für present perfect (z. B. already) und für simple past (z. B. Monday morning) mit unterschiedlichen Farben. Wenn keine Signalwörter vorhanden sind, überlege dir, welches passen würde.

3 WORDS Last week in Victoria Park

Last week there was an open-air theatre in Victoria Park. Sally and I wanted to go there. So we went by Tube. It was good that we could use the travelcards. We were very excited, because it was a criminal story. When it started, a young man came into a room. For a moment we were shocked because he pulled out the plug so that the room was dark. Then a second man came in. He pressed a button and the light went on again. I liked him because he looked so friendly. After the play an interviewer from a newspaper asked us about our opinion of the play. I told him that I liked it because the ending was a big surprise. I won't tell you the whole story! You must go and watch it yourself!

Lerntipp **Wörter einsetzen**

- Lies dir zunächst den Lückentext durch.
- Sieh dir dann die Wörter im Kasten an.
- Setze die Wörter ein, die einfach für dich sind und streiche sie durch.
  So behältst du einen Überblick über die Wörter, die dir noch zur Verfügung stehen.

MEDIATION

Autumn in London

Dein Onkel Ich habe hier ein Angebot in London gefunden. Es scheint sich um ein 3-Sterne-Hotel zu handeln. Aber viel mehr verstehe ich nicht. Ist ein Flug dabei und was steht da über die Hotelzimmer?

Du Man muss den Flug selbst organisieren./ Der Flug ist nicht dabei. (1P) Die Zimmer haben ein Fernsehgerät, Telefon und ein eigenes Bad. (1P)

Dein Onkel Wie sieht es mit der Verpflegung aus – welche anderen Mahlzeiten gibt es außer dem Frühstück?

Du Es gibt Frühstück und Abendessen. (1P)

Dein Onkel Sie schreiben etwas über Aktivitäten am Abend. Gibt es auch ein organisiertes Abendprogramm?

Du Nein, aber sie besorgen Eintrittskarten z.B. fürs Theater, Musical (1P) und sie organisieren den Transport. (1P) Man kann aber auch abends in der Hotelbar bleiben. (1P)

Dein Onkel Jetzt mal zu den Preisen. Ich sehe, dass es unterschiedliche Preise für drei oder vier Nächte gibt, das ist klar. Aber was bieten sie eigentlich zusätzlich an, wenn man vier Nächte bleibt?

Du Bei vier Nächten hat man zwei Halbtages- und zwei Ganztagesbesichtigungsprogramme. (1P)

Dein Onkel Und was bedeutet das Sternchen?

Du An diesen Terminen servieren sie ein spezielles Abendessen bei Kerzenschein am zweiten Abend des Aufenthaltes. (1P)

Dein Onkel Wo findet man etwas über das Besichtigungsprogramm?

Du Du musst hier diese Maske ausfüllen / Du musst hier deinen Namen, Adresse, Telefonnummer und E-Mail-Adresse angeben. (1P) Dann schicken sie dir weitere Informationen zu. (1P)

Lerntipp So kannst du **Mediation Skills** üben:

- Markiere in den Fragen des Onkels **Schlüsselwörter (key words)** – das sind die Informationen, nach denen der Onkel fragt und nach denen du auf der Website suchen musst.
  Ist ein Flug dabei und was steht da über die Hotelzimmer?
- Überlege dir, auf welche englischen Wörter du im Text achten musst, um etwas zu Flug und Hotelzimmer zu finden.
  flight – (hotel) room
- Suche nun gezielt nach diesen Wörtern im Text. Dort wirst du die gesuchte Information finden.
  flight: You organize your flight to London ... ▸ Der Flug ist nicht dabei.
  room: Rooms include TV, telephone, private bathroom ▸ Die Zimmer haben Fernsehen, Telefon und ein Badezimmer.

SPEAKING

03 Talking to Dad

04 Now you

Father	Hi Josephine, good to see you home again. How was your afternoon at the *Underage Festival*?
Josephine	Hi Dad, it was great. (1P)
Father	Who did you go with?
Josephine	I went with Sally, Tina and Lesley. (1P)
Father	Hm. Now, how did you get to London?
Josephine	Well, we went by train. (1P)
Father	And when did the train leave?
Josephine	It left at 1.30 (1P)
Father	How did you find your way to Victoria Park?
Josephine	We went by Tube. We had an underground map. Look, here. (1P)
Father	Which line did you take?
Josephine	We started at Bethnal Green and took the Central Line Eastbound. (2P)
Father	I see. Well, how much was the ticket for the festival?
Josephine	It was great, it was free! (1P)
Father	Oh that sounds good! Come on, tell me more about the festival.
Josephine	The festival was for kids from 14 to 18. We had juice and water. Other drinks weren't allowed. There was great music. We could listen to reggae, rock and electronic music. (3P)
Father	It seems you really had a good time there. And now the most important question: when did you get home?
Josephine	Oh Dad, no more questions, please. (1P)

Lerntipp So kannst du **Speaking** üben:

Präge dir die Antworten von Josephine aus dem Lösungsvorschlag ein, indem du sie mehrmals laut aussprichst. Wiederhole dann die Aufgabe.

Lösungen A

READING

SCOTMAG – your magazine for Scotland

1 About going to school

Bilder, die mit einem Häkchen versehen sein müssen:

Taxi ✔; Deutschbuch ✔; Fähre ✔; Menschen im Bahnhof ✔; Schulbus ✔;

Schüler, die mit dem Fahrrad zur Schule fahren ✔

2 The shortest journey to school

Alice: 4 Leo: 2 Joel: 1 Janet: 3

3 More about the article

	Right	Wrong	Not in the text
1 Every morning Alice goes to school by ferry.		✔	
2 Leo misses his friends in the morning.	✔		
3 Leo's father picks him up after school.			✔
4 Joel is quite happy with his journey to school.	✔		
5 Janet likes going by train.	✔		
6 The four students like school a lot.			✔
7 The magazine is looking for information from students in other countries too.	✔		

LANGUAGE

1 WORDS John Bennet, Isle of Flotta

a)

John Bennet lives on the Isle of Flotta. He is a farmer and works on a salmon farm. When he is out with the boat, his wife and his daughter Alice often feel lonely. Once a month the family visits Alice's great-grandmother Glenna Bennet in Kirkwall on Mainland. They must take the ferry to Mainland. The departure of the ferry is early in the morning. As you can imagine, Glenna Bennet always waits for the arrival of her family. Sometimes John and his family can't visit Glenna – then she is very upset.

b)

great-grandmother:

My great-grandmother is my mother's grandmother / is my grandmothers's mother.

timetable:

A timetable shows you when the bus/ferry leaves / gives you information about the bus/ferry times.

A timetable shows you the different lessons at school / gives you information about lessons at school.

2 WORDS Find the words.

1 I have invited six guests to my party – I expect six guests.
2 Joe is a good friend – he is a good mate.
3 If you can't talk to a person on your mobile, you can send a text message.
4 If you have learned your new words, you know their meaning.
5 Tonight I want to write in my diary – I want to make an entry.
6 If you put the letters in the boxes from 1–5 in the right order, you get a word for an exercise that you sometimes do in your English lesson: translation

Lerntipp So kannst du **Vokabeln üben**:

Nimm die sechs Wörter aus der Übung. Notiere in deinem Lernheft jeweils den ersten und den letzten Buchstaben der Wörter:
Für *expect*: e t
usw.
Schließe dein Lernheft für eine Weile. Schlage nun deine Notizen wieder auf und fülle die Lücken zwischen Anfangs- und Endbuchstaben. Schreibe die deutsche Übersetzung daneben.
Auf diese Weise kannst du in kleinen Lernpäckchen weitere Vokabeln der Unit üben und dir dabei die Schreibweise gut einprägen.

3 GRAMMAR What would happen if ...

1 If Alice lived in Kirkwall, she would sleep longer on Mondays.
2 Leo would go by bus if his father didn't have a taxi.
3 If Joel's parents moved to another part of the town, Joel would be very unhappy.
4 Janet could learn her German vocabulary on the train if she forgot to learn it at home.
5 Janet would be late if she missed the train to Edinburgh.
6 If I lived on the Isle of Hoy, I would go to school in Kirkwall. (= mögliche Lösung)

Lerntipp So kannst du **Bedingungssätze Typ 2 (conditional sentences type 2)** üben:

Die Struktur lässt sich mit der folgenden Übung leicht einprägen.
Du kannst sie schriftlich oder mündlich machen:

Nimm den ersten Satz der Übung als Ausgangssatz:
If Alice lived in Kirkwall, she would sleep longer on Mondays.

Ergänze diesen Satz bei jedem erneuten Sagen oder Aufschreiben um ein bis drei Worte.
Das können auch humorvolle Ergänzungen sein, z. B.

1. If **the funny girl** Alice lived in Kirkwall, she would sleep longer on Mondays.
2. If the funny girl Alice lived in **little** Kirkwall, she would sleep longer on Mondays.
3. If the funny girl Alice lived in little Kirkwall, she would sleep longer on Mondays **and Wednesdays**.
4. If the funny girl ...

Wie viele Ergänzungen schaffst du?

Lerne den Ausgangssatz auswendig. In der Klassenarbeit kannst du dir den Satz gut in Erinnerung rufen und hast so ein Beispiel mit der richtigen Struktur:
if-Satz: simple past – Hauptsatz: would/could + infinitive

STUDY SKILLS

USING A DICTIONARY More information about Joel

1 Joel interessiert sich für den <u>Weltraum</u>.

Joel is interested in <u>space</u>. (1P)

2 Er liest viele Bücher über dieses <u>Thema</u> und <u>sucht</u> <u>Informationen</u> <u>im Internet</u>.

He reads many books on this <u>topic</u>/<u>subject</u> and <u>looks for</u> <u>information</u> <u>on the internet</u>. (4P)

3 Letzte Woche <u>hielt</u> er <u>sogar</u> einen <u>Vortrag</u> darüber.

Last week he <u>even</u> <u>gave</u> <u>a talk</u> about it. (3P)

Lerntipp **Mit dem Wörterbuch arbeiten:**

> ... best before ...
> **Haltbarkeitsdatum** best-before date
> **halten 1** *Verb mit Obj* ◇ hold*; ***er hielt sie an der Hand*** he was holding <u>her</u> hand ◇ *in Zustand, Versprechen, Tier* keep*; ***hältst du dein Wort?*** are you going to keep your word? ◇ *Rede* make*; *Vortrag* give* ◇ *von Torwart* save

Das Beispiel zeigt dir, dass zwar zunächst das Wort *„hold"* angegeben wird. Für den Ausdruck *„einen Vortrag halten"* benötigst du jedoch das Verb *„give"*, das erst weiter unten im Zusammenhang angegeben wird.

> **Information** information; *Informationsschalter* information desk; ***die neuesten Informationen*** *Pl* the latest information *Sg* (⚠ *im Englischen immer Singular*); ***eine ~*** a <u>piece</u> <u>of</u> information, <u>some</u> information
> **informieren 1** *Verb mit Obj* inform; in

Das Beispiel zeigt dir, dass erst in der dritten Zeile darauf hingewiesen wird, dass es im Englischen *„information"* nur im Singular = Einzahl gibt. Überprüfe, ob du in deiner Lösung tatsächlich *„for information"* und nicht *„for information~~s~~"* geschrieben hast.

Lies die Seiten 136 und 137 im Skills File deines Englischbuches nochmals aufmerksam durch.

Bearbeite dann die Aufgaben in den gelben Boxen jeweils am Ende der Seiten. Die Lösungen dazu findest du auf S. 27 im Lösungsheft.

Das Nachschlagen im Wörterbuch wird leichter, wenn du das Alphabet gut kennst.

Die folgende Übung soll dir dabei helfen. Ordne diese Liste von 10 Wörtern alphabetisch:

smile, smell, snake, smoke, shoe, shoulder, shout, share, survey, surprise

Du findest die Lösungen auf S. 27 im Lösungsheft.

WRITING

An e-mail to SCOTMAG

possible opening sentence | possible opening sentence

Dear SCOTMAG,

I think your magazine is really cool. / Hey, what a cool magazine for teenagers. (2P) Yesterday I read the article "Going to school" in your magazine. (1P) I enjoyed it very much (1P) because I learned a lot about teenagers in Scotland. (1P)

first paragraph and what your e-mail is about

Now here is some information about myself: (1P) my name is ... I'm 13 (1P) and I come from ..., a village/town/city in Germany. (1P)

second paragraph

I want to tell you about my journey to school. (1P) I have to get up at 6 o'clock every morning, (1P) because my journey to school is quite long. (1P) The bus takes about 25 minutes. (1P) I like my journey to school, (1P) because I can talk to my friends. (1P)

third paragraph

I will tell them about your article. (1P) It's a good idea for our school magazine. (2P)

fourth paragraph

Will you write about my journey to school in your magazine? (2P)
I hope you will. (1P)
Yours ...

last paragraph and closing sentence

! **Noch ein Hinweis:** In diesem Lösungsvorschlag beginnen die Abschnitte 1–3 jeweils mit einem *topic sentence*. Dadurch kannst du deinen Text noch besser strukturieren und hilfst dem Leser, deinen Text leichter zu erfassen.

Lerntipp So kannst du **Writing** üben:

- Vergleiche deine Lösung mit der Musterlösung. Versuche auf diese Weise herauszufinden, wo du fehlerlos formuliert hast und wo du möglicherweise Fehler gemacht hast (Rechtschreibung, Satzstellung, richtig verwendete Zeiten usw.). Wenn du dir bei manchen Stellen nicht sicher bist, bitte deinen Lehrer / deine Lehrerin um Hilfe.
- Fertige dann eine Berichtigung deiner Lösung an.

LISTENING

05 A presentation about Pitlochry, Scotland

Rick

Hello everybody, I'm going to talk about Pitlochry – a pretty country town in Scotland. First there will be some information about geography. Then I will talk about Pitlochry and tourism, and in my last point I'd like to inform you about special events in Pitlochry.

Please have a look at this map of Scotland first. You can find Pitlochry right in the heart of Scotland. There are 2,500 people who live in Pitlochry. This picture shows you Pitlochry with the nice hills all around and the old stone houses. Well, it still looks very much the way it was 100 years ago, don't you think?

Let me come to my second point: Pitlochry and tourism. Tourists really are very important for the people in Pitlochry. Many tourists come to Pitlochry every year. You can stay in a hotel or a bed and breakfast place. There are also holiday apartments. Look, this is the famous Rosemount Hotel. As I said before, Pitlochry is in the heart of Scotland, so it's the perfect place to explore the Highlands. Many visitors want to see the famous "Salmon ladder". It helps the salmon on their difficult journey. Sometimes the visitors are even able to see a salmon.

Finally, let me come to my last point: special events in Pitlochry. They are the reason for many visitors to come to Pitlochry. Every year in September you can be the guest at a Scottish event for old and young people – the Highland Games. You can listen to bagpipe bands, watch dancing groups and of course you can watch competitions in all kinds of Scottish sports. All year round there is the Pitlochry Festival Theatre with lots of attractions like theatre plays, games and a lot of fun. It's a highlight and many people from all over the world come to visit Pitlochry because of this festival.

1 The presentation

(1) A, (2) F, (3) C, (4) B, (5) H, (6) E; D und G gehören nicht zum Hörtext.

2 Come and spend your holidays in Pitlochry

1 Pitlochry is
2 Pitlochry looks
3 Many people come
4 You can explore the Highlands
5 Come and see
6 The Pitlochry Highland Games
7 If you come to Pitlochry,
8 People from all over the world

a) our famous salmon ladder!
b) if you are staying in Pitlochry.
c) to visit Pitlochry every year.
d) come to the Festival Theatre.
e) you will meet people from all over the world.
f) in the heart of Scotland.
g) a bit like 100 years ago.
h) to stay in caravans.
i) are an attraction for old and young people.
j) if you want to go snowboarding.
k) you will dance a lot.

3 Information about Pitlochry

1 At the beginning of his presentation Rick gives information about	the number of hotels in Pitlochry.	
	the structure of his presentation.	✔
	the youth hostel in Pitlochry.	

2 In Pitlochry	there are stone houses.	✔
	there are 2,800 people.	
	there are 3,500 people.	

3 Visitors to Pitlochry	can stay in a caravan.	
	never stay at hotels.	
	can stay at a Bed and Breakfast.	✔

4 If you visit the Pitlochry Highland Games,	you can watch Scottish sports.	✔
	you need an entrance ticket.	
	you will come in August.	

LANGUAGE

1 WORDS Just the opposite

1 remember ◂▸ forget

2 arrival ◂▸ departure

3 above ◂▸ below

4 small ◂▸ huge (big, large)

5 begin ◂▸ stop (finish)

Lerntipp So kannst du **Vokabeln wiederholen:**

Gegensatzpaare eignen sich gut, um Vokabeln zu wiederholen.
Lege dir am Ende deines Lernheftes eine Liste mit „opposites" an und ergänze sie, immer wenn du auf ein Gegensatzpaar stößt.

2 WORDS In town

a)

buildings, places	traffic
station	street
cathedral	cars
square with a column	rush hour
post office	train
shops	platform
bridge	bus
cinema	bus stop
extra: community hall, church, supermarket	extra: public transport, car park

! Hinweis: Für jedes Wort gibt es einen halben Punkt.
Du kannst dir auch die volle Punktzahl geben, wenn du *bus stop, platform* und *car park* unter der Überschrift "buildings and places" eingeordnet hast.

b)

At the station you can get on a train / get off a train / pick up a friend / ...

At the post office you can buy stamps / ...

At the cinema you can watch films / ...

Lerntipp **Beispielsätze**

Beispielsätze mit den neuen Wörtern der Unit findest du jeweils in der dritten Spalte des **Vocabulary** auf S. 159–180 in deinem Englischbuch. Wenn du also ein neues Wort lernst, präge dir auch immer gleich den passenden Beispielsatz mit ein.

3 GRAMMAR Jason from Pitlochry

Mögliche Lösungen:

1 If I lived in Australia, I would go surfing every day.

2 I would invite my family for a trip around the world if I had enough money.

3 If Manchester United played in Pitlochry, I would buy tickets for the game.

4 I would take a photo of Nessie if I could see her.

Lerntipp **Conditional sentences type 2 (Bedingungssätze Typ 2: Was wäre, wenn ...)**

Lies nochmals die Regeln für die **conditional sentences** in deinem Englischbuch auf S. 151. Anschließend kannst du dich überprüfen und die „Can you"-Aufgabe bearbeiten. Schreibe die Sätze in dein Lernheft. Stelle sicher, dass du im if-Teil des Satzes **simple past** und im Hauptteil des Satzes das **conditional (would/could + infinitive)** verwendet hast.

4 WORDS Last year in Pitlochry

a)

1 Last year I was able to spend three weeks in Pitlochry because I had saved a lot of money.

2 With our holiday group we went to the Highland Games and there we were able to listen to the best bagpipe groups.

3 When I stayed at the holiday camp last year, one day I was allowed to go to a Scottish school.

4 One evening my friends and I were allowed to watch a good film at the cinema.

Now you

b) *Mögliche Lösungen:*

1 Next year I will be allowed to go to Frankfurt by train.

2 Next year I will be allowed to go to a disco.

3 Next year I will be able to meet my friend in Berlin.

4 Next year I will be able to speak English a lot better, because I have the Klassenarbeitstrainer. ☺

Lerntipp **be able to / be allowed to**

Lies die Box *„können"* und *„dürfen"* in deinem Englischbuch auf S. 170. Halte dann einmal die deutschen und einmal die englischen Sätze zu und übersetze sie.

MEDIATION

Tickets for Pitlochry Festival Theatre

Deine Mutter Ich habe jetzt die Veranstaltung angeklickt, für die ich Karten kaufen will. Und was mache ich jetzt?

Du Du musst die Preiskategorie wählen und eingeben, wie viele Karten du kaufen willst. (3P)

Deine Mutter Ah, jetzt sehe ich eine Liste mit den Karten. Aber Mensch, ich hab ja die falschen angeklickt! Kann ich das nochmal rückgängig machen?

Du Ja, du kannst nochmal zurückgehen, wenn du etwas ändern willst. (2P)

Deine Mutter Gut, noch mal von vorne ... Ja, das sind jetzt die richtigen Karten. Jetzt möchte ich mir gerne noch Plätze aussuchen. Wie mache ich das?

Du Du kannst keine bestimmten Plätze aussuchen/buchen – du bekommst automatisch die besten Plätze, die frei sind. (3P)

Deine Mutter Gut. Und wie gehts jetzt weiter?

Du Zuerst musst du deine persönlichen Daten eingeben und wie du bezahlen willst. Dann drückst du auf „Buy tickets" – das bedeutet „Karten kaufen". (4P)

SPEAKING

06 Booking tickets on the phone

07 Now you

Mögliche Lösung:

Lady Pitlochry Festival Theatre booking office, hello. How can I help you?

You Hello, this is *(your name)* speaking. I'd like to book tickets for a play at the Festival Theatre. (3P)

Lady OK. What play are you interested in?

You A Bad Mistake. (–)

Lady And when would you like to come?

You We will be in Pitlochry in March. So we'd like to come on March 27th. (3P)

Lady I'm afraid there are no tickets left for this date. What about another day?

You Well, we could also come on March 1st. (2P)

Lady Let me see, yes, you're lucky. There are some tickets left for this date.
There are tickets for £15.50 and £22. Which tickets would you like to take?

You We'll take the tickets for £15.50. (2P)

Lady OK. How many tickets do you need?

You Two, please. (1P)

Lady Can you spell your name, please?

You Yes, that's ... and ... (4P)

Lady Thanks. The tickets are waiting for you at the theatre. You pay for them when you pick them up.
Is that OK for you?

You Yes, thank you very much. Goodbye. (3P)

Lady You're welcome. Bye-bye.

Lerntipp So kannst du **Speaking** üben:

- Präge dir die Antworten aus dem Lösungsvorschlag ein, indem du sie mehrmals laut aussprichst. Wiederhole dann die Aufgabe.
- Nimm dir lange Namen oder andere Wörter vor und übe an ihnen das Buchstabieren. Falls du dir das englische Alphabet in Erinnerung zurückrufen willst, kannst du es auf S. 229 in deinem Englischbuch nachschlagen.

READING

Sports and English – teenage holiday camps

1 What is the brochure about?

The brochure is about ...

... teenagers in a British summer camp.	
... learning English in an outdoor summer camp.	
... summer camps where you do lots of sport activities and learn English.	✔
... how sporty students spend their summer holidays in England.	

Lerntipp **Umgang mit Lesetexten**

Um längere Lesetexte leichter zu verstehen, ist es sehr hilfreich, sich zu Beginn einen Überblick zu verschaffen, um was es überhaupt geht. Dann kannst du auch unbekannte Wörter leichter erschließen. Bevor du also mit dem intensiven Lesen anfängst, überfliege den Text anhand
- der Überschrift,
- der Zwischenüberschriften,
- der Bilder,
- des ersten Satzes jedes Abschnitts.

2 Susanna is interested in the camp

1 The camps are in Germany/Freiburg, Rostock, Munich and Dresden.
2 The teenagers come from all over Germany.
3 They sleep in tents.
4 In the camp you are not allowed to smoke, to drink alcohol or to take drugs.
5 You learn English in small groups / special courses.
6 In the English courses they listen to English radio news / watch English films / read the newspaper / talk / discuss / sing. *(zwei Angaben)*
7 The teachers speak English and German.
8 After the second day you tell them what you are going to concentrate on / choose your sports activities.
9 You can go surfing in Rostock only.

Lerntipp **Sätze vervollständigen (Completing sentences)**

Meist sind mehrere Lösungen möglich. Überlege daher immer, ob es vielleicht noch eine weitere – einfachere – Lösung gibt, bei der du ganz sicher bist, dass sie sowohl inhaltlich als auch grammatikalisch richtig ist.

LANGUAGE

1 WORDS Camp activity: football

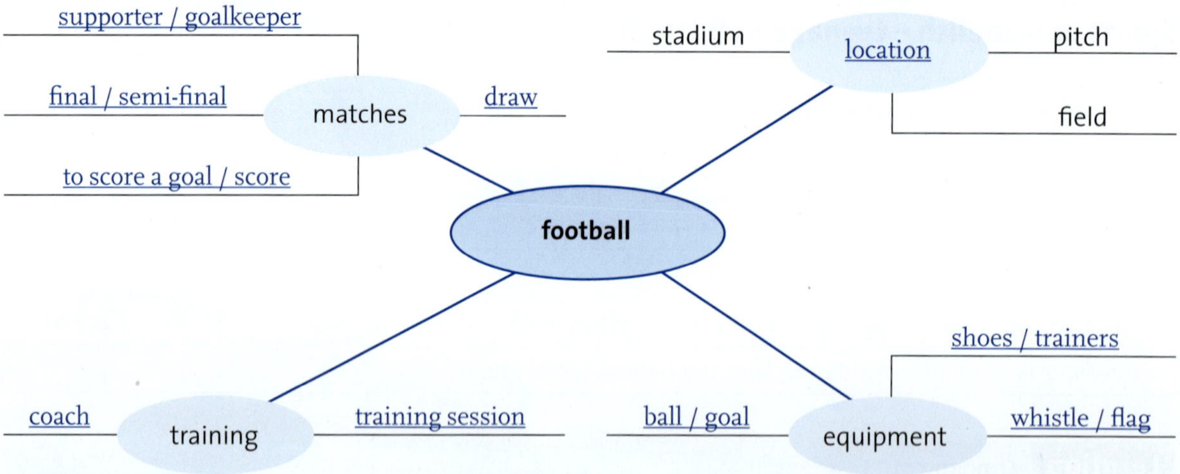

Lerntipp **Sports and vocabulary**

Auf der folgenden Website findest du viele Anregungen zum Thema Sport und Wortschatz, unter anderem auch ein Quiz, in dem du deinen Wortschatz zum Thema Fußball überprüfen kannst: www.englishclub.com/vocabulary/sports-football.htm

2 WORDS More sports

a)

sport	equipment	location
badminton	badminton racket	court
swimming	swimming trunks / swimsuit	pool
skateboarding	helmets / pads / skateboard	half-pipe
table tennis	table tennis bat	sports hall

b) *Mögliche Lösungen:*

You go swimming / you swim in a swimming pool. You need swimming trunks / a swimsuit.

You play badminton on a court. You need a badminton racket.

You go skateboarding on a half-pipe. You need a helmet and pads.

3 GRAMMAR Susanna and the camp

a)

1 Susanna is a student who comes from Freiburg.

2 Susanna is the only student who came to the camp by bus.

3 Tennis and football are the two activities that Susanna chose on the third day.

4 Aerobics is a sport that many girls in the camp chose as their favourite activity.

5 Mike is the English teacher who always starts the lesson with a song.

6 Nate is the only boy who chose aerobics.

b) *Mögliche Lösungen:*

1 Frank is a student who comes from Hamburg.

2 Basketball is a sport that many kids chose/choose on the third day.

Lerntipp **Relative clauses** (Relativsätze)

- Lies das Grammar File 4 in deinem Englischbuch auf S. 152.
- Bearbeite die „Can you ...?"-Aufgabe auf derselben Seite.
- Schreibe dazu die Sätze in dein Lernheft. Markiere mit zwei unterschiedlichen Farben, die Person oder die Sache, auf die sich **who** oder **that** beziehen.
- Entscheide dann, ob du **who** oder **that** einsetzen musst.

c)

Nr. 3 und Nr. 4

Lerntipp **Contact clauses** (Relativsätze ohne Relativpronomen)

So findest du heraus, ob du **who** oder **that** weglassen kannst: Du musst **who** oder **that** verwenden, wenn es direkt vor einem **Verb** steht:
Susanna is a student **who comes** from Freiburg. ▸ **who** kann nicht weggelassen werden.

STUDY SKILLS

PARAPHRASING Susanna is getting by in English

a)

1 Trainer — It's somebody who trains a sports team.

2 Friseur — It's somebody who cuts your hair.

3 Gemeindehalle — It's a place where people from a village / a town can meet and have parties, concerts, ...

4 Durchsage — It's something that you can hear at an airport or a station.

5 Helm — It's something that you must wear on your head when you ride a bike.

6 Bahnsteig — It's a place at the station where the train arrives and leaves.

b)

1 coach 2 hairdresser 3 community hall

4 announcement 5 helmet 6 platform

MEDIATION

Papa Wer kann sich überhaupt um eine solche Unterstützung bewerben?

Du Familien mit drei oder mehr Kindern. (2P)

Mama Wie viel Geld steht insgesamt zur Verfügung und wie viel könnten wir als Familie bekommen?

Du Insgesamt stehen 5000 € zur Verfügung, wir könnten höchstens 200 € bekommen. (2P)

Papa Welche Angaben muss man bei der Bewerbung machen?

Du Um wie viel Geld wir uns bewerben wollen, (0,5P) Name, Adresse, Anzahl der Kinder in der Familie, (0,5P) Name und Datum des Camps (0,5P) und wie viel Geld wir im Monat zur Verfügung haben. (0,5P)

Mama Muss man der Bewerbung sonst noch etwas beilegen?

Du Ja, ich muss einen Aufsatz darüber schreiben, warum ich am Camp teilnehmen möchte. (2P)

Papa Wann müssen wir uns bewerben?

Du Spätestens bis zum 1. Mai. (1P)

Mama Und wie geht es dann weiter?

Du Wir müssen auf die Antwort warten, das kann manchmal drei oder vier Wochen dauern. (2P)

Papa Kann man da jedes Jahr einen neuen Antrag stellen?

Du Nein, man kann nur jedes zweite Jahr einen Antrag stellen. (2P)

Papa Gibt es sonst noch etwas Wichtiges, was wir wissen sollten?

Du Ja, im Camp wird niemand erfahren, dass wir eine solche Unterstützung bekommen haben. (2P)

SPEAKING

08 Getting to know the other teenagers at the camp

Now you

Mögliche Lösung:

Name	Katrin
Age	14
Where from	
– town/city/village	Überlingen
– where in Germany	in the south of Germany, on Lake Constance[1]
Brothers or sisters	no brothers or sisters, a lot of cousins
School	
– languages	English, French
– favourite subjects	Art, Biology
– …	school drama club, last play: "Emil und die Detektive"
What he/she wants to be	nurse
Why here at the camp	wants to get better in English and likes sports
Favourite sport	swimming; goes swimming every day
Sport he/she wants to do at the camp	volleyball
+ why	wants to join the volleyball team at her school

You

Hello everybody. This is Katrin. (1P) She is 14 years old and she comes from Überlingen. (1P) That's in the south of Germany, on Lake Constance. (2P) Katrin hasn't got any brothers or sisters but she has got a lot of cousins. (2P)

At school she learns English and French. (2P) Her favourite subjects are Art and Biology. (1P) She is also in the school drama club. (1P) Their last play was "Emil und die Detektive". (1P)

One day she wants to be a nurse and work in a hospital. (2P)

Katrin has come to the camp because she wants to get better in English and she likes sports. (2P)

Her favourite sport is swimming. (1P) In the summer she goes swimming in the lake with her friends every day. (2P)

Here in Freiburg she wants to do volleyball because she wants to join the volleyball team at her school. (2P)

Lerntipp So kannst du üben einen **freien Vortrag** zu halten

- Bevor du den von dir gewählten Schüler vorstellen kannst, musst du dir unbedingt ausreichend Notizen machen, damit du deinen Kurzvortrag später flüssig halten kannst.
- Schreibe nicht jedes Wort auf, das du sagen willst. Dein Vortrag wird nur dann echt, wenn du frei sprichst und nicht bereits auswendig gelernte Sätze vorträgst.
- Halte deinen Vortrag öfter und sprich dabei laut. Finde Zuhörer, die dir eine Rückmeldung geben können über deine englische Aussprache, deine englische Grammatik und deine Vortragsweise. Versuche dann die Hinweise in deinen weiteren Vorträgen zu beachten.
- Wenn du einen aufnahmefähigen MP3-Player oder ein Mikrofon / eine Webcam am Computer hast, kannst du dich selbst aufnehmen und dann deinen eigenen Vortrag überprüfen.

[1] Lake Constance [ˌleɪk ˈkɒntstənts] *der Bodensee* [2] nurse [nɜːs] *Krankenschwester/Krankenpfleger*

Lösungen B

LISTENING

9 A visit to the Lowry

Man

Why not visit the Lowry with your family? There is so much to see and to do there. It's a great place to visit for everybody in the family. There are all kinds of activities waiting for you in the Lowry. Your kids will love the Lowry from the first step they take into the museum.

Woman

You want to see the famous paintings of the painter Lowry with your family? At the information desk of the museum there are rucksacks waiting for you. In the rucksacks you will find games, puzzles and activities that will help you to explore the building. Whenever one of your children says: "Mummy, paintings are boring", you simply open the rucksack again and take out another game or even a short activity.

Boy

Hi, I'm Dave. It was fun to walk round the museum with the rucksack. We stopped here and there and had a look in the rucksack. I remember that we were standing in front of one of Lowry's paintings and we had to find things like a dog and a man with a green hat in the painting. It was me who saw the dog first. Dad was second.

Man

Or join our workshops. This month you can design your own postcards or join the story-telling workshop. Next month there will be many drama activities for everybody in the family.

Girl

Hello, this is Sara. Last Sunday my sister and I made postcards in one of the workshops. My postcards were all funny, my sister made some birthday cards. Now we are sending them to our friends.

Man

You will like my last point: from 12 November to 31 March we have "Free Family Sundays" so families don't pay. So why not invite your family for a cup of tea in the museum's restaurant? See you soon!!

1 About the advert

The advert is about …

… the address of the Lowry.	
… the painter Lowry.	
… going to the Lowry with the whole family.	✔
… the times when you can visit the Lowry.	

2 About the Lowry

The Lowry is	only open for families.	
	a good place for families.	✔
	only for small children.	

The rucksacks	are a great help for families.	✔
	are not allowed in the museum.	
	are good for food and drinks.	

Next month there will be	a drama workshop.	✔
	activities for telling stories.	
	postcards with Lowry's paintings.	

In December	there are no workshops.	
	families don't pay to visit the museum.	
	Sundays are free for families.	✔

In the Lowry	you can go to the restaurant.	✔
	you can buy postcards.	
	you must have a rucksack.	

3 At home

1 games, puzzles, activities *(es genügen zwei Angaben)*

2 design your own postcards, join the story-telling workshop, drama activities *(es genügen zwei Angaben)*

3 families don't pay

STUDY SKILLS

PARAPHRASING Talking about the Lowry

Mögliche Lösungen:

An artist is someone who draws pictures/paintings.

The "Free Family Sunday" is a day when families needn't pay. / a day when families can get into the museum for free.

The Lowry is a place/museum where you can look at the pictures/paintings by L. S. Lowry.

The creative workshops are something where you make things.

The story-telling workshop is something where you come together and tell stories.

LANGUAGE

1 GRAMMAR More information about the Lowry

a)

1 Children under 10 are the visitors who like the story-telling workshop best.

2 The rucksacks are an attraction that most families like.

3 Mr L. S. Lowry was an artist who was born in Manchester.

4 Every month there are new workshops that you can join.

5 The drama workshops are the workshops that women between 25 and 45 like best.

b)

2, 4, 5

Lerntipp So kannst du **contact clauses (Relativsätze ohne Relativpronomen)** üben:

- Lies den Relativsatz mit Relativpronomen laut. Meistens hörst du dann schon, ob das Relativpronomen **who/that** weggelassen werden kann.
- Lies das Grammar File 5 **contact clauses** auf S. 153 in deinem Englischbuch durch.
- Bearbeite dann die „Can-you ...?"-Aufgabe auf derselben Seite.

2 WORDS Find the words

1 Put the letters in the correct order.

2 I've had these flowers since last year – they are artificial.

3 Peggy had an accident with her bike – we had to call the ambulance.

4 She had an operation on her knee.

5 Larry is a good goalkeeper.

6 This summer our team won the championship.

7 I love sports like running and jumping – I love athletics.

Lerntipp **Wörter lernen**

So kannst du den Schwierigkeitsgrad beim Lösen dieser Aufgabe erhöhen:
Bearbeite die Wortschatzübung mit etwas zeitlichem Abstand ein zweites Mal.
Decke dann die Kästchen ab – die Schwierigkeit erhöht sich, wenn du nicht weißt, wie viele Buchstaben das gesuchte Wort hat.

WRITING

A day out to the Lowry

Art is great (2P)

We, the students of Form 7 LM, went on a day out to the Lowry in Manchester on February 25th. (2P)

We were in the museum from 10 am to 2 pm. (1P) The building is really amazing. (1P)

We want to do a presentation about the famous painter L. S. Lowry, (2P) so we tried to find out as much as possible about him. (2P) The people at the museum helped us to collect lots of information. (2P)

We also copied one of Lowry's paintings. (1P)

It was very interesting because we did different games and activities around the paintings. (2P)

Some students even designed their own postcards. (2P) They look fantastic. (1P)

It was a great day out and I think it is a good idea for school classes to go there too. (2P)

Lösungen zu den Aufgaben der Lerntipps

Unit 2 STUDY SKILLS Using a dictionary

Lösung zur Aufgabe im Englischbuch S. 136

1	at your own risk	auf deine (eigene) Gefahr
2	'rose'	stieg auf
3	'rises'	geht auf
4	blow up	in die Luft jagen
5	voice	Stimme
6	jn.	jemand
7	Obj.	Objekt
8	PL	Plural
9	USA	United States of America

Lösung zur Aufgabe im Englischbuch S. 137

1 difficult, hard

2 heavy

3 serious

4 difficult, hard

5 serious

6 heavy, violent

Lösung zum alphabetischen Ordnen der Wörter

share, shoe, shoulder, shout, smell, smile, smoke, snake, surprise, survey

Lösungen A

READING

Alexander von Humboldt (AvH) German International School Montreal

1 What is the website about?

This website tells you about …

… how you can find online friends at a Canadian school.	
… how German and Canadian schools work together.	
… what the school offers to students.	✔
… how parents and students prepare the Open House.	

2 About AvH

1	I	2	H	3	F	4	A	5	G	6	D

3 More details about AvH

1 from different countries

2 at the kindergarten

3 German, French, English

4 they have book nights

5 they go on study trips

6 the building, the classroom, the science and art rooms, the library

LANGUAGE

1 WORDS A school discussion

1 Twenty years ago family life in Canada was very traditional.

2 Parents were strict and children had to help a lot in the house.

3 Today family life is very modern in many ways.

4 My parents are easy-going, but sometimes a bit old-fashioned.

5 Many parents disagree with their children about how long they should be allowed to watch TV.

6 You can't blame the children for modern technology.

7 Children should know exactly how long they are allowed to play computer games.

8 One hour per day in front of the computer is enough.

2 GRAMMAR Information for the school camp

a)

1 The students will be allowed to bring their guitars but they won't be allowed to bring their MP3 players.

2 They will be allowed to play football and volleyball but they won't be allowed to play before breakfast.

3 The students won't be allowed to smoke or drink alcohol.

4 They will be able to spend some time alone or with friends.

5 The students won't be allowed to stay away from the camp for more than an hour.

6 They will be able to make new friends and talk to them in German.

b) *Mögliche Lösungen*

We were allowed to listen to music.

We were allowed to make a fire in the evening.

We weren't allowed to bring our mobile phones.

We were able to / allowed to buy some ice cream.

We were able to go swimming.

We were able to play table tennis.

3 GRAMMAR Open House at AvH School

The Open House on 16 March was a really exciting day at Alexander von Humboldt School. My class met – at 8 am with our form teacher Mrs Silver. She wanted to show the visitors how we prepare – / ourselves for tests. Before the lesson started I asked myself if this would be interesting for our visitors. But it was! First we felt – a bit strange. But it was OK later.

Form 8 HD presented their project "First steps in the kitchen". They have learned how to cook – / themselves some easy meals. Another project showed how you can protect yourself from a bear.

Simon from Year 9 showed some of his exciting skateboarding tricks and told the visitors that he had taught himself how to skateboard.

I think that all the visitors enjoyed themselves at our Open House. So the day was worth getting up so early.

Lerntipp **Reflexive pronouns (Reflexivpronomen)**

Lies das Grammar File 8 in deinem Englischbuch auf S. 155 durch. Bearbeite dann die Can you ...?-Aufgabe auf derselben Seite.

4 GRAMMAR Activities at AvH

a)

Year 7 is visiting a museum on 5th April.

Year 8 is going to Germany in June.

Years 3 and 4 are having a sleepover at school at the weekend.

Year 1 is visiting the zoo on 15th May.

Year 6 is going on a trip to the country next week.

Lerntipp Über **feste Pläne und Verabredungen** reden

- Lies das Grammar File 7 auf S. 155 in deinem Englischbuch.
- Bearbeite dann die Can you ...?-Aufgabe auf derselben Seite.

b) *Mögliche Lösungen*

Überprüfe, ob du in deinen Lösungen das present progressive (am/are + ...ing) und eine Zeitangabe für die Zukunft verwendet hast *(on Friday, next week, at the weekend, tomorrow, ...)*.

My friend and I are going to the cinema next Saturday afternoon.

I'm cooking a meal for my family on Saturday.

I'm going on a bike ride together with my friends tomorrow.

I'm revising for my next Maths test on Friday.

My sister and I are visiting our grandma on Sunday afternoon.

WRITING

An e-mail about a school trip

Dear friends,

Today we want to tell you about our trip to the Black Forest last month. (1P)

We met at the station at 6 o'clock in the morning. (2P) Although we were still very tired, we were really excited. (2P) Then we got on the train and went to our youth hostel in the Black Forest. (2P) We arrived there at about 10.30 am. (1P)

The hostel was really big and nice but the people who worked at the hostel were very strict. (3P) We weren't allowed to stay in our rooms from 9 am to 6 pm! (2P) But the food that we got in the hostel was delicious!!! (2P) Our teachers were easy-going – we were allowed to go to the village alone and to stay up until 11 in the evening. (2P) We even had a super disco on our last evening. (1P)

Write back soon and tell us about your last trip. (1P)

Love, Form 7a (1P)

Lerntipp So kannst du deine **Lösung für eine Writing-Aufgabe überarbeiten:**

- Überprüfe, ob du folgende Punkte beachtet hast und hake sie ab:

Checkliste	
• Brief/E-Mail: Anrede, Grußformel? • Bericht/Geschichte: Überschrift?	
• alle wichtigen Punkte aus der Aufgabenstellung beachtet?	
• 1–2 einleitende, interessante Sätze am Anfang (ohne Details)?	
• Text mit Paragraphen (Abschnitten) logisch strukturiert?	
• abwechslungsreicher Wortschatz? (Adjektive, Adverbien, treffende Verben)	
• unterschiedliche Satzstrukturen? (Relativsätze, Sätze mit linking words)	
• Rechtschreibung, Grammatik (Zeiten und Wortstellung!) OK?	
• haben deine Sätze eine sinnvolle Länge? (keine Endlossätze „ohne Punkt und Komma“)	
• Brief/E-Mail: Schlussformel? • Bericht/Geschichte: Schlusssatz?	

- Nachdem du diese Punkte überprüft hast, erkennst du, an welchen Stellen du noch nacharbeiten musst. Gib nicht zu schnell auf – gewöhne dich vielmehr daran, deine Entwürfe mehrmals zu überarbeiten. (Das ist bei Menschen, die beruflich Texte schreiben, übrigens völlig normal.) Lies in Zukunft erst nach mehreren Überarbeitungen die Musterlösung in diesem Heft.
- Wende dein Wissen zum Schreiben und Überarbeiten eines Textes doch gleich noch auf eine weitere Writing-Aufgabe an. In der Klassenarbeit B findest du auf S. 56 eine zusätzliche Writing-Aufgabe. Gutes Gelingen!

Lösungen B

LISTENING

10/11 New contest at Radio CBC 1, Montreal

10 1 Kids' Club on Radio CBC 1

Radio speaker

Hey kids, welcome to the Kids' Club on Radio CBC 1. I hope you're all in good form today. Some of you already know that each year we hold a national contest for you. It is an art and writing contest for all kids from 6 to 16 years. Now, what is this year's contest about? Well, we know you all love Canada. If we want to save the beauty of our country, we have to protect it. We can protect it if we save energy. So this year's topic is about saving energy. How can we Canadians do that?

We are sure you have a lot of ideas for posters, reports, stories or poems. Some of you are even great artists. So why not paint or draw something? With your ideas you can help make Canada cleaner, healthier and a better place to live. It's your chance to be creative and win a great prize.

You need more information or ideas? Look at our website and ask your teachers. They will tell you everything about our prizes too.

Send us your work by 30th April.

Good luck and have fun!!

a)

One class is writing a diary about their two-week camp near Ontario.	
One class is making posters about how people can use public transport more often and in this way help to keep the air of our country clean.	✔
One class is working on a musical about the life of young people in Canada.	

b)

1c, 2b, 3c, 4a

11 2 At Victoria School, Toronto

Mrs Riley

Today I want to tell you a bit more about the rules of the contest "Saving energy".

If you write a report, a story or a poem, please use the computer. You mustn't write more than three pages and your work must have a title. You are not allowed to simply copy things from the internet, from books or magazines of course. If you draw or paint something, make sure you use the right size of paper. You can only use white paper. Please find a title for your work and write it down clearly on the back of your drawing or painting. You can work in groups of no more than three students.

The school will send all the results to Radio CBC 1. The last day to hand in your work here at school is 20th April.

Now, have you got any more questions? Yes, Sarah?

Sarah

We haven't talked about the prizes. Can you tell us something about them, please?

Mrs Riley

Oh yes, I forgot the most important thing! Everybody who joins the contest gets a small present. Then there will be three winners from every school, eight winners from every province and finally there will be fifteen national winners. The prizes are cameras, cellphones and books for the school and province winners.

The prizes for the national winners are two-week camps in all parts of Canada. So get started, do a good job and – win.

a) Mrs Riley is talking about ...

	Yes	No
the rules for writing.	✔	
when they can use the computer room.		✔
when they can talk to their Art teacher.		✔
the rules for painting and drawing.	✔	
what students have to do in class and at home.		✔
the prizes.	✔	

b)

1 use the computer / don't write more than three pages / have a title for your work (4P)
(Zwei Angaben genügen.)

2 to copy from the internet, books, magazines. (3P)

3 20th April (1P)

4 two-week camps in all parts of Canada. (2P)

→

Lerntipp So kannst du üben, **Fragen zu einem Hörtext zu beantworten**:

Lies die Fragen vor dem Hören und markiere dir in jeder Frage Schlüsselwörter, die dir helfen, die gewünschte Information herauszufiltern.

Hier sind die Schlüsselwörter markiert:

1 What is important when you want to write something?
2 What are you not allowed to do?
3 By when do you need to hand in your work at school?
4 What are the prizes for the national winners?

Benutze diese Technik, wenn du bei einer Listening-Aufgabe Fragen beantworten musst.

LANGUAGE

1 WORDS Paraphrased words

1 It's something you find in a theatre: stage
2 It's something you get when you want to pay in a restaurant: bill
3 After you have written a text or a story and you want to make it even better, this is what you do: revise
4 It's something you might come through when you're canoeing: rapids
5 It's a person who is a boss: leader

2 WORDS Free time in Canada

a)

1 You can go hunting.
2 You can go swimming.
3 You can go snowboarding.
4 You can go canoeing.
5 You can play hockey.
6 You can have sleepovers.

b) *Mögliche Lösungen:*

1 Last February Year 7 went snowshoeing in the mountains.
2 Last July Year 8 played hockey.
3 Last September Year 1 had a sleepover at school.
4 Last October Year 11 went hunting.
5 Last June Year 6 went canoeing.
6 Last August Year 9 went swimming in a lake.

3 GRAMMAR Lunch break at Victoria School

1 The girl is talking to herself.

2 Two girls are teaching each other Maths.

3 Two girls are hiding themselves from the camera of a boy.

4 One boy is making himself a sandwich.

5 "I can see myself in the mirror," the girl at the table says.

4 GRAMMAR Anna and her Canadian friend Janet

1 Almost every week they write e-mails to each other.

2 They both want to learn Spanish, but they can't take Spanish at school.
So they have got a Spanish book and a CD. They are teaching themselves Spanish.

3 Sometimes they even chat with each other in Spanish.

4 Today Anna wants a photo of Janet and Janet wants a photo of Anna.
So they take photos of themselves and send them to each other via e-mail.

Lerntipp **themselves** or **each other?**

Lies dir in deinem Englischbuch das Grammar File 9 auf S.156 durch. Bearbeite dann die Can you...?-Aufgabe auf derselben Seite.

5 GRAMMAR Working for the contest

1 On Monday Pete and Joel had to interview the people in the city of Toronto.

2 On Tuesday Amy had to draw pictures of buses in Toronto.

3 On Wednesday Amy and Joel had to talk to students about school buses.

4 Today Pete and Joel will have to write the report and Amy will have to find pictures for the report. (2P)

5 On Friday they won't have to work on the report.

Lerntipp **be able to / be allowed to / have to**

- Schlage im Grammar File 6 auf S.154 in deinem Englischbuch nach und vervollständige diese Tabelle:

Hilfsverb	Ersatzverb in der Grundform (Infinitiv)	Form für die Vergangenheit	Form für die Zukunft
can *(können)*	be able to		
must			
may, can *(dürfen)*			

- Bearbeite dann die Can you ...?-Aufgabe auf S.154 in deinem Englischbuch.

MEDIATION

A contest in Germany

Phil I'm interested in your contest. Is it right that everybody must write a report about PE at your school?

You Well, you can write a report but you can do other things too.

Phil So, what are the other things? (4 things)

You You can also write a story, a poem, make an interview or a poster. (4P)

Phil That sounds interesting. Who can you interview then?

You We can interview a student from our school who has got a favourite sport. (2P)

Phil And how are you going to send them the interview? (2 things)

You We can make a soundfile or write it down. (2P)

Phil What is the first prize?

You You can win a ticket for one year for their football club. (2P)

Phil Oh, I'd like to win a ticket like that. Who can work on the contest?

You Everybody from 10 to 16. (1P)

Phil I'd like to make a poster. What are the rules for the poster? (2 things)

You It must be about PE at school and we must use colours. (2P)

Phil What about you? Could we work together?

You Yes, of course, we can. (1P)

Phil So, what are we waiting for? Let's go.

WRITING

Great sports day at ... School (1P)

Last Saturday our school had a special sports day. (2P) We wanted to collect/get money for some outdoor sports equipment for our school. (3P)

Every form prepared an activity. (2P) The younger children had fun with table tennis and our school's special water games. (2P) There were football matches for the older children. (2P) Some of the teams played really well, but in the end a team from ... (name of a school) School won. (2P)

Most parents enjoyed a cup of tea or coffee and some sandwiches. (3P) The day was super and in the evening we had enough money for the sports equipment. (3P)

Lerntipp So kannst du **Writing** üben:

Wenn du deine Writing-Fertigkeiten wirklich verbessern möchtest, musst du häufig daran arbeiten. Die Überprüfung anhand der Checkliste auf S. 31 im Lösungsheft ist ein wichtiger Schritt, den du immer machen solltest.
Möchtest du noch eine weitere Aufgabe zum Üben? Hier sind weitere Vorschläge:

Schreibe für ein kanadisches Jugendmagazin:
- Write about your favourite sport.
- Write a report about an interesting football match.
- Write a story. Use the following words: hockey – last Friday – hospital.

SPEAKING

12 An interview for the contest

13 Now you

Phil Hello Alexander. Thank you for taking time for this interview. Just tell me a little about yourself. How old are you, where are you from?

Alexander OK. I'm ... years old and I'm from ... , that's a city/town/village near ... (2P)

Phil Right Alexander. Tell me, what sport do you do in your free time?

Alexander Well, my favourite sport is skiing. (1P)

Phil And I've heard that you are already very good at it, aren't you? When did you win your last contest and what kind of contest was it?

Alexander In January I won the contest of all the schools in this area. (3P)

Phil And have you already been to national contests?

Alexander Well, I've been to one of these contests in the Black Forest, on the Feldberg. That was last year. (3P)

Phil And did you win?

Alexander No, I didn't win a prize but I came sixth, which is really good. (3P)

Phil Tell me when did you start skiing?

Alexander I learned skiing from my mum and dad when I was six and I liked it from the beginning. (3P)

Phil And how often do you train?

Alexander In winter I train every weekend and in the holidays. Maybe I'll train more next year. (3P)

Phil Well, I wish you all the best, perhaps you'll even come to Canada for a contest one day. Thank you very much for the interview.

Lerntipp So kannst du dich **auf eine Speaking-Aufgabe vorbereiten:**

- Mit Hilfe von Notizen kannst du dich gut auf eine Speaking-Aufgabe vorbereiten. Du hast die Möglichkeit, deine Gedanken festzuhalten und sie immer wieder zu ergänzen oder zu verbessern. Das gelingt natürlich besonders dann, wenn du ungefähr weißt, worüber das Gespräch gehen wird. Dann kannst du in deinen Notizen Stichworte möglicher Fragen eintragen und dir dann deine Antworten zusammenstellen.

Lösungen A

READING

An article for TEEN MAGAZINE

1 STUDY SKILLS Skimming

Mögliche Lösungen:

... what you can do to prepare yourself for the fashion school.

... what you can do to get into a fashion school.

... what Simon has found out about how to become a fashion designer.

2 Susanna needs information

2 ✔, 3 ✔, 6 ✔, 7 ✔, 8 ✔, 10 ✔

3 About Simon's article

1c, 2a, 3c, 4c, 5b, 6a

LANGUAGE

1 WORDS An alphabetical list

a)

A	ecnuanon	announce	N		
B	**isabgppe**	bagpipes	O	eotpear	operate
C	earrce	career	P	eipp	pipe
D	gwaidnr	drawing	Q		
E	dretoi	editor	R	erdidl	riddle
F			S	escuscs	success
G	og ornwg	go wrong	T	uent	tune
H	dohhaeensp	headphones	U	suulfe	useful
I			V	**noaatcvi**	vacation
J			W	ewka pu	wake up
K	peke	keep	X		
L	reehlat	leather	Y		
M	**aiucsnim**	musician	Z		

b) movie, article, biography, caption, least, silence, section, successful, company, capital letter, tense

c) *Mögliche Lösungen:*

1 Bagpipes are a famous Scottish instrument. / Bagpipes are an instrument that is famous in Scotland.

2 A musician is a person who plays an instrument well. / Katie Melua is a famous musician.

3 Vacation is the American word for holidays. / Vacation is a time when there is no school for days or weeks.

Lerntipp **Wörter wiederholen**

Mit einer A–Z-Liste lernst du eine weitere Möglichkeit kennen, Wörter zu wiederholen. Finde ein Thema, das dich interessiert, z. B. Kleidung, Sport, ... und versuche einfach, bei jedem Buchstaben ein Wort einzutragen. Für Lücken in deiner A–Z-Liste kannst du dein Englischbuch oder ein Wörterbuch zu Hilfe nehmen. Ergänze diese Wörter mit einer besonderen Farbe. So fallen sie dir gleich ins Auge und du kannst sie nochmals gesondert lernen.

2 GRAMMAR At a London fashion school

1 In July, Jimmy is reading some books about the history of fashion.

2 In June, Sue is making clothes for going out.

3 From July to September, Vivian is working in a clothes company.

4 In July and August, Lisa is doing a course in drawing.

5 In August, Ian is visiting France.

Now you

Mögliche Lösungen:

1 In July, I'm staying at my grandma's for two weeks.

2 In August, I'm going to a summer camp.

3 In my summer holidays, I'm reading the latest Harry Potter book.

Lerntipp **Über Pläne und Verabredungen reden**

- Bearbeite die Can you...?-Aufgabe in deinem Englischbuch auf S. 155.
- Welche festen Pläne oder Verabredungen hast du für das Wochenende? Berichte deinen Eltern / deinem Bruder / deiner Schwester / einem Freund / einer Freundin auf Englisch davon. Achte darauf, dass du das *present progressive* und eine Zeitangabe verwendest.

MEDIATION

A Canadian family in Germany

Your mum Frag sie, wie lange sie schon in Deutschland sind und wie lange sie noch bleiben.

You How long have you been in Germany and how long are you staying here? (2P)

Woman We have been here for two weeks and we are staying until the end of the month.

You Sie sind seit zwei Wochen hier und bleiben bis zum Ende des Monats. (2P)

Your mum Frag sie, wo sie hier wohnen.

You Where are you staying? (1P)

Woman We are staying in a small holiday apartment. It's small but we like it very much. It's good because we can cook our own meals. So we needn't go to a restaurant every day.

You Sie wohnen in einer kleinen Ferienwohnung. Sie ist klein, aber sie gefällt ihnen sehr gut. Es ist gut, weil sie da auch ihre Mahlzeiten kochen können. So brauchen sie nicht jeden Tag ins Restaurant zu gehen. (3P)

Your mum Frag sie mal, ob sie noch Ideen für Ausflüge brauchen.

You Do you need any more ideas for trips? (2P)

Woman Well, we have seen quite a lot of this area really. We want to visit one or two museums. Can you give us an idea where we could go?

You Also, sie haben sich hier in der Gegend schon recht viel angesehen. Aber sie möchten noch ein oder zwei Museen besuchen. Sie möchte wissen, ob wir ihr da noch Ideen geben können. (3P)

Your mum Wie wäre es, wenn wir die Familie in den nächsten Tagen zum Kaffee zu uns nach Hause einladen? Dann können wir ihre Pläne besprechen und werden etwas Gutes finden. Und ich backe einen guten deutschen Kuchen.

You My mum wants to invite you to our house for a cup of coffee. Then we can talk about your plans and will find something good for you. And my mum will make a good German cake. (3P)

Woman Thank you so much. We would like to come and of course we all like German cake.

LISTENING

14 At Brandon's office

Brandon Hello?
Mitsu Hi, Brandon, this is Mitsu. How is it going?
Brandon Hey Mitsu, nice to hear from you. Well I'm working on our new magazine again. It's going to be really good. We will have some good stories in the sports section about fitness, you know, exercises that keep you fit, and then rugby and a report about a girls' football match. Just imagine: one of these girls scored three goals in the first half.
Mitsu Wow, that's amazing.
Brandon Now, what about your movie section, Mitsu?
Mitsu There is one article I'm not sure about. I mean, I don't know if the article will be interesting for our readers. A boy called Paul wrote something about a Chinese film he had seen in New York. Apparently he thought it was really cool. But the problem is that the film isn't on in Canadian cinemas.
Brandon I see, but I'm sure it'll be OK. Let's discuss this on Friday afternoon. Is that OK for you?
Mitsu Yes, it's fine, see you on Friday then, bye.
Brandon Bye Mitsu.

Brandon Hello?
Jeff Hi, this is Jeff Miller speaking. Could I talk to Robert, please?
Brandon Hello Jeff. I'm afraid Robert is only here in the office on Friday afternoons. Can I help you?
Jeff Well, I've just written a report about a brilliant concert our school choir gave, and I wanted to ask if he was interested in it for the music section of TEEN MAGAZINE.
Brandon Why don't you call him at home, Jeff? His number is 63913641.
Jeff Thanks a lot, bye.

Brandon Hello?
Lisa Hi this is Lisa speaking. Am I talking to Brandon?
Brandon Yes, you are, Lisa. How can I help you?
Lisa I have this idea for a new section "Jobs and career" for TEEN MAGAZINE. You know everything that has to do with how to find the right job, which school to go to, but also about successful learning for school and this sort of thing.
Brandon That sounds really good, Lisa. Could you come to my office some time this week? Let me see, what about tomorrow afternoon at about 4?
Lisa Yes, I'd like to come.
Brandon Fine – and bring along all the articles that you've got so far, all right? Bye then.

Nathalie Hello?
Brandon Hi Nathalie, this is Brandon. I just wanted to ask you about the fashion section. Have you got enough good articles for the next edition?
Nathalie Yes, I think so. First there's a report about school uniforms in different countries. I think it's super. Then there is a survey about what to wear at the beach this year. We will see a lot of colourful bikinis. And I found a funny poem about socks. I'm sure you will like it.
Brandon Oh, about socks, how exciting. Will you send all the material by Friday, please?
Nathalie You will have it tomorrow. OK? See you.

1 HEADLINES in the next TEEN MAGAZINE

5 minutes that will keep you fit	✓
Latest films at Toronto cinemas	
My visit to a cinema in New York	✓
A first-class concert 50 students sing	✓
An interview with a pilot	
Great fashion show at high school	
Susan – queen of girls' football	✓
When did YOU last go to the cinema?	
A report about Maths at school	
A report about my favourite singer	
Power learning	✓
THIS YEAR AT THE BEACH	✓
101 socks	✓

2 About the calls

a)

1c, 2b, 3a, 4b

b)

1, 5, 6, 7

LANGUAGE

1 WORDS An article in TEEN MAGAZINE

Becoming a star

Hi, my name is Michael Howell and I'm 15 years old. I'm quite a good singer and I can play the guitar well. When you play a musical instrument, you always dream of a big career as a musician. Sometimes I already see my name in bold print in the newspaper together with a photo and a caption: "Michael Howell – a story of success".

So when I heard about an audition for a new CD with songs from local teenagers I went there. I had to go to the office of the company first and tell them some facts about myself. That was for a short biography. Then the big moment came: I went into the studio and played and sang two songs. They recorded them. They will tell me in a few days if one of my songs will be on the CD. I hope that I was successful. They will release the CD in summer. So keep your eyes open – I think it will be sold out soon.

2 Getting by in English

1 Keep your eyes open.

2 That's up to you.

3 I think she/he has a crush on you.

4 I'm good at Maths.

WRITING

1 Correcting mistakes

My favourite star is a man. He was born in England in 1982. When he was five years old he **got** his first guitar from his father. He started to play and soon he was quite good. He learned to sing too. His friends liked his music. Very often they asked him to play at parties. When he was 18 he played his first concert and at the age of 22 **he released** his first CD. It was a success.

Lerntipp **Richtig schreiben**

Lege dir eine persönliche Fehlerkartei an, von Fehlern, die du oft machst. Notiere dabei auch, wie es richtig heißen muss. Wenn du einen Text schreibst, dann benutze diese Fehlerkartei als persönliche Checkliste.

2 New editors for TEEN MAGAZINE

Mögliche Lösung:

Dear Brandon,

I'm a reader of TEEN MAGAZINE and I think it's great. All of my friends like it too.

My name is Nina. I'm 14 years old and I live just outside Toronto.

My hobby is riding my bike, so I'd like to open a new section "Everything about bikes".

I think there are a lot of things that we can write about in this new section: a report about different types of bikes, tips about how to repair your bike and of course many ideas about where to go on bike tours.

Please contact me if you like my idea. Here is my name and address:

Nina Sullivan, 24 Park Ave, Toronto, phone number: ...

SPEAKING

Brandon's answering machine

Now you

Mögliche Lösung:

First caller:

Hi Brandon, this is Caitlin Callahan speaking , that's C-A-I-T-L-I-N C-A-L-L-A-HA-N.

We have got an appointment for Thursday, 14th July, at 5 pm. I'm afraid I can't come because I have to go to the doctor.

Could you please call me back so that we can make a new appointment? Thank you. My number is ...

Second caller

Hello Brandon, my name is Myron Heath, that's M-Y-R-O-N H-E-A-T-H.

I have a question. I've written an article about my last visit to California, USA. I'd like to know if you want to publish this article. Please call back. My number is ...

Third caller

Hi Brandon, this is Michael. I have got more information about the two young Germans who were in Montreal last month. The name of one of them is Matthias Winterhalter, that's M-A-T-T-H-I-A-S W-I-N-T-E-R-H-A-L-T-E-R, and his number is ... Matthias is waiting for your call. Bye Brandon.